PRAISE FOR *FRENCH FRY LEADERSHIP*

"Anyone who is managing or preparing to manage people at any level (especially the restaurant business), should read this book. I've known Bruno for thirty years, and the thoughts and messages in this book are truly how he lives his life. As a Burger King franchisee for thirty-five years, I've had the privilege of observing his philosophy, operations, and the successes of which he speaks. This book clears up the misconception many people have of the meaning of many forms of management."

—**Steven Sobieski,** President, Statny Foods, Inc.

"Can you supersize my order with an extra copy of *French Fry Leadership* to pass on? If Michelin gave stars for leadership, Bruno would be a multiple-star winner. The simple wisdom that permeates this fast and easy-to-read book is critical reading for anyone in a leadership capacity. Stocked with stories and examples of fundamental concepts that are valuable for any supervisor or manager, it's a winner. Go buy a Whopper and read some of the sagest wisdom I've ever read on how to treat people, treat customers, and show that whatever level you are, you can always step up and help out when needed."

—**Howard H Prager,** Leadership Consultant and Author of *Make Someone's Day: Becoming a Memorable Leader in Work and Life*

"Bruno's wise experience motivating entry level staff to do amazing things has helped me in my business. We have many frontline folks we can't afford to pay more but who are critical to our team and client experience. Bruno's advice has helped me motivate them to strive for higher goals and take pride in their work. This has resulted in better client service and retention. I feel it's caring enough to pay attention to the employee's needs and wants. Everyone talks about it. Few do it. Thanks, Bruno, for your help and inspiration."

—**John McKay,** CEO, Healthcare Venture Partners

"This book is brimming with excellent advice and counsel for managers at all levels of organizations both large and small. My father, a successful manager, always said that if you take care of quality and people, other aspects of the enterprise will take care of themselves. Bruno translates that philosophy into excellent practices throughout this volume. His counsel is logical, practical, and doable. That is not to say it's easy, however. A good manager must constantly be on the alert to ensure their actions are in line with their words. Every person who aspires to be a great manager would benefit by reading the book."

—**Roger Breisch,** Speaker

"I am very fortunate to count Bruno as one of my mentors in leading people and am pleased to see a small sliver of his leadership knowledge distilled into a very approachable set of concepts for everyone. He has a gift of making people feel valued through his actions and truly walks the talk in this book. If you are looking to be a better leader in any arena, I highly recommend this book."

—**Steve Schreiner,** Entrepreneur

"Found this book to be of great interest as it brought up so many points on how to develop a successful team and how to value their contributions to the organization. The book . . . goes in depth on how people respond to leadership when leadership shows a willingness to listen to coworkers. The book is an easy read that I think everyone will enjoy. Remember, good managers don't need to let underperforming people go; they will leave on their own. Also, people want to work when they feel part of the team."

—**Bill Borrelli,** VP National Accounts, Darling International

"If you want to learn how to lead a team the correct way, this book is a must-read. There is a lot of gold in this book that needs to be applied to today's workforce."

—**Tim Edwards,** Owner, Omni Containment

"It's an easy read and it pulls all facets of wise leadership into one volume. Motivating workers at a fast-food restaurant or any other business can be a daunting task. Or is it? This book shows you how."

—**Dave Heun,** Journalist, Editor, and Writer

"A strong organization and successful leadership is a function of the consistent application of universal standards that bring unbridled commitment from staff at every level. This book does a great job of diving into how a leader can create this type of culture throughout their organization."

—**Ray Rogina,** Mayor of St. Charles, Illinois (2013–2021)

French Fry Leadership: How to Attain Profits through Serving People

by Bruno Hilgart

© Copyright 2023 Bruno Hilgart

ISBN 979-8-88824-006-9

All rights reserved. No part of this publication may be reproduced, stored in a retrieval system, or transmitted in any form or by any means—electronic, mechanical, photocopy, recording, or any other—except for brief quotations in printed reviews, without the prior written permission of the author.

Any trademarks referenced within are the intellectual property of their respective owners.

Published by

3705 Shore Drive
Virginia Beach, VA 23455
800-435-4811
www.koehlerbooks.com

FRENCH FRY LEADERSHIP

How to Attain Profits
Through Serving People

BRUNO HILGART

WITH ADITYA SHEKHAR

VIRGINIA BEACH
CAPE CHARLES

TABLE OF CONTENTS

Foreword (by Laurie Roscoe) 1

Foreword (by Aditya Shekhar) 5

Introduction 7

What I Did for a Living 9

What is Management 15

Taking Care of the Numbers through Taking Care of People 17

Management Culture 21

Managers Should Eliminate Speed Bumps, Not Create Them 25

I Have Never Fired Anyone 29

Love What You Do or Learn to Love What You Do 35

A Good Employee is Not Always a Good Manager 39

How to Coach 43

Leaders Are "On Stage" 47

Be the Employer of Choice 51

Words and Definitions Matter 55

Stress the Why behind Everything 57

Communication Is the Oil in Relationship Engines 61

Where to Leave Problems (The Suitcase Theory) 65

The "Better Job" Myth 67

Consistency Sells 71

People Quit Bosses, Not Jobs 73

In the Skill of Management, Failure to Train
Is Training for Failure 75

Don't Assign Something You're Not Willing to Do 79

Partner with Your Partners 83
The Importance of Passion.. 87
Being a Problem Solver versus a Problem Identifier....................... 91
The Importance of Being Humble 95
Guest Recovery... 99
Confirming It All 105
Dedication 109
Special Acknowledgment to Aditya Shekhar 113

FOREWORD
(BY LAURIE ROSCOE)

I first "experienced" Bruno Hilgart in 1989 as a newly promoted manager in the fast-food business. My biggest memory of our first meeting was thinking, *What the . . . heck?* At that point in my life, I had never come across an individual with quite that much positive energy, and I was not sure what to make of it.

Bruno and I had similar pasts. We both lived on the wrong side of a wealthy and well-to-do city outside Chicago with old-school parents. A good day was when you made it through without getting slapped for looking at a parent in what they considered the "wrong way." Passion for anything besides next weekend's party was not on the radar.

Bruno taught me that we were not just slapping burgers and fries together to get people in and out as quickly as possible; we were managing million-dollar profit centers in a world where new places to eat in our neighborhood were popping up at an alarming rate. And we couldn't do it alone. We had to create and motivate a winning team to make it happen—in an industry paying minimum wage for what is considered a "dead-end job."

Bruno instilled the concepts discussed in this book into our daily operations. We made a positive difference in people's lives. This happened for both our employees and customers. Obstacles were removed, needs were provided for, and communication was top-of-the-line. Our team members were shown their importance on a daily basis, and no one stood in their way. In other words, they were given the freedom to succeed.

Bruno taught me to pass on the credit to the team when things went well. And, when things didn't go as well as planned, we—as leaders—needed to step up and take accountability. This approach resulted in us having a thriving, award-winning company with extremely low turnover and employees that genuinely enjoyed what they did. We were educated, motivated, and ready to make miracles happen. We were a winning team, and I almost felt guilty collecting a paycheck because work was enjoyable.

Throughout the years, we continued to grow as a result of the motivated individuals that felt truly valued by their employer. We were honored to be a well-respected small company. Our parent brand would routinely approach us for feedback or ideas, and we would be called upon to help other franchisees because we had a demonstrated track record of success.

I had many wonderful work years until Bruno left the company. Then, all of a sudden, I found myself sitting in his chair. Only later did I learn that he had been secretly preparing me for this position. He constantly exposed me to tasks and situations that were beyond my job description for enrichment and ongoing training. I could do anything I wanted now because I was the "top dog," and I called all the shots.

In my new role, I first began looking for ways to make changes to the organization, but I learned I didn't have to. I quickly realized that the right culture was already in place. All I needed to do was just continue it. If it ain't broke, don't fix it.

And our stores soldiered on until it was time for our little success story to become part of a much bigger restaurant operating franchise. While many things are different, one will remain the same. The beliefs, values, and culture that was built through Bruno's leadership carries on, and we are lucky enough to have a big new pool of people to share it with.

I will be forever grateful to Bruno for what I learned during the twenty-seven years I spent working with him. He inspired me, made me realize how important I was, and gave me the confidence to handle any situation that came up. Knowing he was there to teach and coach me gave me peace of mind as I climbed the ranks. I was going to learn and move onward and upward, all with his support. This read is worth your time if you're interested in building a strong culture where production is top-notch, turnover and missed work is low, and profit goals are exceeded!

FOREWORD
(BY ADITYA SHEKHAR, COAUTHOR)

Over the last few years, I've probably taken hundreds of rideshares and met some incredibly fascinating people. There's the budding musician, the self-proclaimed workaholic, the jovial retiree looking for an excuse to get out of the house, and even a minor celebrity (that's a story for another day). However, none were more captivating than Bruno Hilgart.

I was flying out of Chicago and needed a ride to the airport. I fired up my smartphone to request a ride and was promptly informed that Bruno (five stars) was a few minutes away. I don't enjoy silent car rides, so I always try to make small talk. You always hear the most interesting perspectives—it might be words of wisdom or directions to a hidden gem restaurant serving Michelin Star–worthy meals at a Discount Tire price.

The ride from my apartment to Midway Airport was probably around forty-five minutes. It was a Friday afternoon, and Chicago's rush hour was in full swing. Bruno started the conversation mildly, making pleasant small talk. I could tell we were getting along, so I inquired a bit further. Bruno told me that he'd been in the fast-food business his whole life. I asked what that was like.

Then he said something that made me pause—"I spent my whole career making people put more passion into salting french fries than they ever thought possible." I had to learn more.

The remainder of the ride, Bruno provided some of the clearest philosophy on management I had ever heard. In that one car ride, I learned more about leading people than I had from full semester-length business school classes. Bruno made things abundantly digestible.

The concepts were so simple. Leaders serve their team members. Managers don't fire bad employees—bad employees fire themselves. Profits come when you put people first. A good employee is not necessarily a good manager. There's a difference between telling and coaching. People quit bosses, not jobs.

I wanted these messages to reach a wider audience. I wanted every leader and manager to hear what Bruno had to say, so I asked him to stay in contact with me. Over the next few years, we put together this book and became friends along the way. There were hurdles and challenges, including our demanding schedules, cross-country moves for both of us, and even a global pandemic. But, looking back on the past three years, I could not be prouder of what we've come up with.

I can say with absolute confidence that Bruno changed my life and how I approach leadership. It is my hope that our words will have a similar impact on you.

INTRODUCTION

When we hear the word profit, most of us think about money. But really, there is so much more to profits than just money. The one takeaway message I want you to leave this book with is that developing people develops profits. These principles will help bring money and profits to your bottom line. However, more importantly, these principles will also have people wanting to work with you. In turn, you will "profit" from the relationships you build with these people. Effective leadership is nothing short of a win-win-win-win for you, your company, your clients/customers, and those who work with you.

WHAT I DID FOR A LIVING

So why learn lessons in management or leadership from me? What experience do I have in leadership? For that matter, what did I even do for a living?

I ask myself this question often. What makes me any kind of leadership expert? I never went to college, and I grew up with just the bare essentials. Among Maslow's hierarchy of needs, I had the basics. I lived in a home with no air-conditioning, a murky river in the front, and a sewage treatment facility just outside of my backyard. Depending on which way the wind was blowing, hot summer nights were not very pleasant. That being said, I had food, clothes, and a roof over my head. My stepdad was a union plumber, and my mother never graduated high school and never held a formal job from the time they got married until I was twenty years old. During the day, she would occasionally stay at the hobby shop my stepdad owned while he worked the plumbing job. This helped us put food on the table during a tough economy from 1977 until 1979.

I learned early on that if I wanted to go somewhere or buy anything, I would have to earn the money myself. So, at the age of twelve, I got the quintessential teenage job: a paper route. Every so often, I challenged myself to make more in tips than I previously did.

To do this, I needed to please my customers however I could. I would give them everything they wanted in the hopes that they would consider me the best paperboy they ever had. If everything went to plan, my goal of increasing tips would be certain. This strategy worked so well that when I left for a better opportunity two years later, I got a number of cards from my customers telling me they didn't want to see me go.

I started my next job right after I turned fourteen. With another friend, I was in the competition for a busboy position at a local restaurant. When the position became vacant, she waited for her stepfather to get home from work and give her a ride to the restaurant while I rode my bike to the restaurant right after school and was hired on the spot. I was paid $2 per hour and received 15 percent of the server's tips. However, I quickly learned that going the extra mile got me a little more than 15 percent.

When I turned fifteen, the first Burger King restaurant was built in my hometown. I always loved their burgers and really wanted to work there. However, they were not hiring anyone under sixteen, so I waited until I was old enough. Immediately after my birthday, I applied with them and was initially turned down. Less than a month later, I begged someone I knew who worked there to put in a good word for me. They finally agreed to an interview and hired me on a two-week trial basis. As it turns out, I ended up working there for thirty years.

Let's get back to the question, "Why me?" I really have no expertise except for all that I've been through in my life, personally and professionally. In many ways, I have tried to be in the right place at the right time and make the best of all the potential opportunities that have been given to me. Once a door opens for us, it's up to us—and only us—what we ultimately do with it. At Burger King, my supervisors liked my work and commitment and knew they could trust me with a task. So, at seventeen, I became an assistant manager, and at twenty, I was running my own restaurant.

I never abused the opportunity or took it for granted. I firmly believe that we are only as good as our last day of work. Throughout my career, I have only missed one day of work—this was because I had to have my appendix removed. While I tried to "schedule" it for my next day off, which was three days away, the doctors told me my surgery simply couldn't wait. I called my assistant manager and moved the schedule around so I could be off for the day of the surgery and two days afterward to recover. I was back to work on day three and did not end up missing any time because the other managers were kind enough to switch shifts with me so I could get those two days off.

As I progressed in my career with Burger King, I was blessed to have the opportunity to attend many seminars and trainings and be exposed to some of the best/most influential motivational speakers in the world. The teachings of these management experts and my own experience on the front lines of the fast-food industry have helped shape my management style. Every manager has a "style," even if they aren't consciously aware of it.

My team members and those around me knew what I did for a living because, to be an effective leader, I needed to set an example in everything that I did. As a matter of company policy and to cultivate a feeling of personal service, we required our team members to wear name tags while working. I took this to heart, and I wore my name tag almost everywhere—from coaching my kids' sports teams to going out with friends or family. If someone caught me outside of work when I wasn't wearing my name tag and asked me what I did for a living, I'd say, "I am responsible for developing teams of people who are more motivated to salt french fries, clean bathrooms, and everything in between more than they ever thought possible when they applied for the position or accepted the job. All for minimum wage."

We were not trying to find a cure for cancer (although, thank goodness people are out there doing this), nor were we laying pipes outside (I'm also thankful people do this because I'm very glad my faucets work).

Our people knew that we were working every day to create a dining, drive-thru, and take-out experience that would cause guests to drive by two McDonald's, a Chick-fil-A, and a Wendy's just to come to our Burger King. Once there, I wanted them and all my team members to ensure that they would bite into a Whopper and say, "Why would I go anywhere else for a fast-food burger ever again?"

Our team members were required to learn critical traits they could use to be successful in any long-term career. These traits certainly helped them in our restaurants, and many of them used these lessons in subsequent careers. These traits included dependability, punctuality, teamwork, guest service, food safety, and even how to work with people they didn't like.

I'm often asked, "What's the return on investment of traits such as these?" The culture at our restaurant fostered real, measurable results with strong key performance indicators (KPIs). Our sales were consistently 20 percent or higher above results for the market, region, and even system-wide. We won the Franchise of the Year award at the 2003 Global Convention, and I'm most proud to report that our turnover was a third of the industry average. The average tenure for our hourly team members was three and a half years.

This success was not because our people were making millions. I would argue our success was because our team members felt valued—their ideas mattered, and they knew that they were part of a team they could feel proud of. In one way or another, they were making a difference—our goal was a *positive* difference—in the lives of our guests. Our principles boiled down to QSCC, which stood for quality, service, cleanliness, and courtesy. We ensured our standards lived up to those values. The temperature of our food, cleanliness of our dining room and restrooms, speed of service, and genuine effort of our team members could never be taken for granted and were nonnegotiable. Our guests came to our restaurants each day with different challenges and things going on in their lives, including work problems, health problems, neighbor problems, relationship problems, boss problems, money problems, and unimaginable problems. We ensured our team members knew the power of genuine smiles, eye contact, and sincere friendliness. Our goal was to help ensure that our guests left our restaurants better than when they arrived, whatever their baseline was. We made sure our team members knew that people sometimes go out to eat just to "get away" from their problems. At restaurants like ours, we had just two minutes and thirty seconds or less in the drive-thru and three minutes or less at the front counter to make a positive difference in our guests' lives.

Emphasizing this helped create what all our team members looked for in their work—a feeling of purpose (something every employee at any company wants). Our employees learned a lot, had fun while doing so, and looked forward to coming to work.

WHAT IS MANAGEMENT?

While there are many aspects to it, management as a concept is, at its core, the ability to get something done through someone else. Understanding what this simplistic interpretation of management means unlocks why so many managers struggle and why their employees are unsatisfied with their jobs. Many of these employees don't dislike the duties of their jobs. They dislike their bosses.

So how and why does this happen? Many times, managers are being internally promoted into a managerial role solely because they were good at the nonmanagement job they previously held. Either the company needs to find management, or the employee may have reached the top of their pay scale and the company is trying to justify paying them more, so the employee gets promoted into management. The employee is rarely going to turn down a pay increase, so they accept the promotion.

In the past, they performed their jobs acceptably—sometimes admirably—but they were just responsible for their own work. As long as they performed their job properly, they were golden. Most managers are promoted from within, and in a management role, they can no longer do all the work by themselves. They have to get things done through others. Many times, they lack the skill to effectively function in this role.

One of the most effective ways we can feel satisfied with our jobs is to see our work produce positive results. Cleaning, for example, is very simple yet very important and can be very rewarding. We can easily see the before and after. Seeing something dirty, unorganized, or disheveled become clean, organized, and well-kept can bring a sense of accomplishment.

Now, how can a manager who's struggling with the management aspect of their job apply this tactic? Everyone knows when a manager is struggling. Their team knows it, they know it, and their clients are likely to catch on. Managers in this situation often revert or regress into doing something with their time that they know how to do and are comfortable doing, usually tasks they performed as regular employees. These managers switch to doing these tasks because they can easily derive a sense of accomplishment and satisfaction from things they have experience doing. In any organization, a manager reverting to old duties—perhaps those already being successfully performed by employees in nonmanagerial roles—is seeking short-term gain for long-term pain from a management standpoint. Failing to address manager reversion is as serious as failing to address a major flaw in your business model and becomes a weakness that can wreak havoc on employee culture.

In many ways, effective management has to be taught. It shouldn't be learned "on the fly"—businesses where managers are figuring out how to manage while on the job are destined to underperform.

TAKING CARE OF THE NUMBERS THROUGH TAKING CARE OF PEOPLE

The fundamental premise behind this book is that taking care of the people ultimately takes care of the numbers. Part of doing this involves servant leadership. Servant leadership is a leadership philosophy that designates the role of the leader as being in service to the organization and all team members they lead.

When leaders passionately work from the heart to serve their people, it creates a situation where team members genuinely want to work as hard as possible and strive to be great in all that they do. Looking at things from the employee perspective, leaders practice servant leadership by providing ongoing feedback, praise, coaching, and attempting to "catch their employees doing things right" by offering opportunities to showcase their work. Servant leaders also manage poor performance swiftly with a positive and fair reaction. Finally, true servant leaders do not look for credit; they pass it on. Servant leadership is unconditional love in a professional setting. It is the belief that a leader's job is to serve those they lead.

Servant leadership—and setting up teams for success with resources—assures that everyone can be on the same page and move forward together. In virtually any industry, having motivated team members willing to put in effort to achieve the organization's goals is a surefire recipe for success. It might seem easy to invest in high-tech equipment or expensive consultants to improve efficiency. While the strategies can be effective, a safe starting point is always the people within an organization—namely, ensuring that they are motivated by the right leadership and have the tools to succeed. No amount of technology or business analysts can compensate for uncomfortable or unmotivated employees working under bad leadership. My philosophy has always been delivering profits through people, and effective leadership is so important when caring for the people who make up an organization.

Being an effective leader who can deliver profits through people requires an understanding of the most important aspect of the equation—the people. Effective leaders should be able to understand the wants, hopes, and needs of their team. Furthermore, they should be dynamic in their leadership in ways that can address these items. Leaders who are perceived as unavailable or unaware of the experiences of their team members will be less able to motivate their employees than leaders who are intimately aware of or (at minimum) show complete respect for what their teams are going through.

Ultimately, top-line and bottom-line results are what truly matter to the short- and long-term success of any business. How well does "taking care of people" translate into "taking care of the numbers"?

Let me give you an example. It was August 1994. Burger King was having major success as a brand after teaming up with Disney and their animated movies of the time. Sales of our growing Kids Club Meals (Burger King's version of the Happy Meal) were booming, which, in turn, drove the sale of more adult meals. Parents were the ones getting kids to our restaurants or, at a minimum, were the ones coming in to pick up these meals. The Burger King brand was having so much success featuring characters from The *Little Mermaid, Beauty and the Beast,* and *Aladdin* that rival McDonald's signed a ten-year exclusive agreement to be the only quick-service restaurant allowed to cross-promote Disney intellectual property. We were forced to go elsewhere, and the brand turned to Disney's competitors, such as DreamWorks.

Having a two-year-old and a four-year-old at home when this all took place, I was in the middle of the affected target market. This gave me the opportunity to get our teams fired up about how to generate buzz around our meals. At this time, I was a general manager, and I was managing two of our nine locations. My turnover and average tenure of my team was the best in the company, so I had a team with experience and successes. I'll describe how I was able to keep top-tier talent later on in the book. My team drove us to record top-line sales and bottom-line profits that were off the charts. My locations set records that were never beaten again in the company's history.

My results blew away expectations while the other seven locations struggled to meet expectations. Bonuses were paid out monthly, and my bonus was more than the other managers bonuses combined—by almost double. I use this story to illustrate that the management ideas and principles that you will read in this book will translate into better results, validating the concept of "as we take care of our people, the numbers will take care of themselves."

MANAGEMENT CULTURE

At some point in their tenure, every manager needs to explore how they want to develop their management and organization cultures. In any organization, culture needs to be understood in real-world terms, and managers are often best served if they take some time to explore what culture means to them and their team. I saw culture as the "vibe" or "feeling" my team had during work.

Every group of people attempting to accomplish something together has a culture. In other words, culture is unavoidable. Organizational and management culture determines how much commitment, focus, and motivation team members apply to their work and how clients perceive the operation of the business. The question all managers should ask themselves when examining their culture is "does the culture work for or against our goals?"

Generally speaking, there are two types of culture: formal culture and organic culture. Formal culture can be described in handbooks, manuals, and mission statements, while organic culture is what's actively practiced by the organization's members, especially their leaders. The worst thing that any of us can do in any relationship is overpromise and under deliver. And yet, when formal and organic culture is not aligned, this is exactly what happens. Discrepancies between formal and organic culture can often arise through bad management. Leaders in all capacities determine the severity of any discrepancies between formal and organic culture by how closely they follow the formal culture. If a supervisor does not believe in or follow the fundamentals of the organization, these discrepancies might be significant. Some discrepancies can be harmless, but too many can impact the team's ability to meet their targets and goals. In these situations, pressure falls on individuals, and employees will adopt an "every man for themselves" attitude. When employees are focused on self-preservation over the organization's goals, genuine caring, respect, and dignity will wane.

Organizational culture can also be undermined through bad leadership, often in the form of cutbacks or increased workloads. Because they have less and less time, employees take shortcuts, and tasks do not get completed. Team members also listen to each other less and do not follow up to ensure important matters are taken care of. In the worst case, team members stop caring entirely about their work because they assume—by their words and, more importantly, their actions—their supervisors do not care.

As you might be able to gather by now, culture can be an extremely powerful force. The challenge for any organization is ensuring that culture becomes a driving force toward goals rather than a hindrance. Strong culture ingrained over decades can orient employees and align them with an organization's goals and specific way of doing things, but it can also serve as a hindrance and even stifle innovation if left unchecked. Stagnant culture often prevents diversification, which has led to the downfall of many businesses with significant market share in doomed industries. Ideally, culture should be dynamic and ever-changing. Organizational culture should not be the master of employees—rather employees should be the masters of the organization's culture.

In my opinion, this was the number one thing we did when managing our restaurants to ensure we didn't have a culture challenge on our hands. And I don't think that this is just applicable to the fast-food industry. Any organization with teams should fundamentally recognize how important the team members are to the culture-generating process. Put simply, involve your people in the creation and decision-making process as much as possible. It's much better to hear feedback about a potential problem from a team member than hear about that same problem (now real) from a client. Businesses spend millions or even billions of dollars each year on consultants, firms, and focus groups to develop culture and brand identity but often ignore some of the best sources of inspiration—their own employees. After all, wouldn't it make sense to hear from, receive feedback from, and solicit new ideas from the people closest to the action?

In our restaurants, whenever we redesigned or updated our team member handbook and policy manual, we involved our nine general managers who were responsible for each location. We carved out fifteen to thirty minutes at every weekly meeting to go through each and every policy or statement in the new iterations of both documents. Even though this process often took months, we were able to achieve a more-than-acceptable level of commitment and consistency in our operational engine. By going through this process, our general managers had faith, trust, and motivation in us and each other. They knew the rationale behind each and every policy and got a firsthand look into the organizational policy-making process. This led to our managers understanding our organizational goals better than they ever had, and discrepancies in organic versus formal culture were at an all-time low. Simply put, we as leaders were all marching from the same tune.

Even if your organization has more than nine manager-level staff, this process is still worth adopting. When every leader is pulling in the same direction, amazing things start to happen. Consistency will be present in every department shift by shift and location by location. When management transfers or internal promotions happen, there will rarely be disagreements about the way things should be done, a problem that currently plagues many multilocation businesses.

Involving managers and employees at all levels into the culture-generating process helped create what is arguably the core and foundation of our business. This foundation, like in any building or skyscraper, needs to be solid, strong, consistent, and dependable no matter what the weather brings.

MANAGERS SHOULD ELIMINATE SPEED BUMPS, NOT CREATE THEM

Earlier in this book, we talked about the philosophy of servant leadership and the idea that a leader's primary role is to serve others. One of the most important things that leaders and managers can do is set up teams for optimum performance in their responsibilities.

Now, what does this look like? Setting up teams for optimum success involves giving them all the tools necessary to complete a task, providing them with the necessary manpower and training, and then—perhaps most importantly—getting out of their way.

Having said that, getting out of our employees' way doesn't mean that we're unconcerned, checked out, or blind to our teams' successes. I cannot stress the importance of managers who cheer on their teams and celebrate their successes. Celebrating successes is a great way to show teams that you are responsive to their actions and are monitoring them without focusing solely on what can be improved. Bosses who only interact with their employees when things need to be corrected are likely to generate resentment and feelings of distrust, which ultimately hinders work and organizational progress.

Managers should solve more problems than they create, but

overmanagement, in many instances, causes additional headaches for employees.

In the world of Burger King, this happened frequently when it came to the drive-thru. There is no denying that the drive-thru dramatically changed the fast-food landscape. In the beginning of the drive-thru era (late 1970s and early 1980s), they accounted for less than 30 percent of overall sales. In 2012, however, they comprised nearly 70 percent of overall sales—in essence, the majority of our guests were not walking through our doors but driving up in their cars.

You'd think, then, that most locations would invest in extensive drive-thru training and ergonomically setting up kitchens and equipment to maximize speed, order accuracy, and guest satisfaction. However, the reality at many drive-thru restaurants was much different. Usually, in most locations, the drive-thru was viewed as an afterthought; perhaps this is because, to many managers, the restaurant aspect was more important, despite sales at the drive-thru being much higher.

For instance, most locations stocked three to four headsets, and it was commonplace for one or two headsets to be broken at a time. In many industries, 25-50 percent of communication equipment being unusable would be a serious concern. Managers simply would not invest in headset repair, instead opting to spend their budgets elsewhere. They would often put off headset repair for months yet still require their teams to maintain the same standards for accuracy and efficiency. This led to demotivated teams, who must work around broken equipment and substandard equipment availability.

In our restaurants, we invested in six to seven working headsets. If a unit or two needed repairs, there were still enough headsets for everyone. We would prioritize repairing broken headsets, and if other items needed tending to, we would try to work with our vendor partners to tackle multiple items. Furthermore, if every headset was working, efficiency was improved dramatically, shaving precious seconds off wait times and improving order accuracy. Managers could wear a headset to monitor radio traffic and the ordering process to give accurate (and hopefully positive if possible) feedback to their teams.

The morale of this story is prioritization and, more importantly, how managers need to understand where the heart of their business truly lies. Simply because they were running restaurants, many fast-food managers focused on the interior experience—what you expect when you think of a restaurant—instead of where the majority of business was actually coming from, the drive-thru. I'm sure there are similar examples in other industries; leaders perceive the heart of their business as one thing, when, in reality, it is something completely different. Managers should go out of their way to examine where the heart of their organization lies and ensure that resources are adequately distributed.

Lastly, let's take a deeper dive into how focusing on and eliminating this speed of service speed bump/pothole paid off for the people and the overall success of the business. By having six or seven working headsets in each of our locations, our top-line sales revenue was markedly higher than the rest of the market. Having our employees and managers dialed into what was happening at the drive-thru at all times led to more productivity and throughput because attention was accurately focused on this important component of our business.

In our market (Chicago, IL), there were contests run to see who could attain the coveted 100 Car Club status. The 100 Car Club was any restaurant that was able to get 100 vehicles (or more) through the drive-thru per hour during lunchtime (we'll say between 11:30 a.m. and 1:30 p.m.).

Even though we only operated 9 of around 270 locations in the Chicago market, we attained this mark more times than any other operator. This—along with other trackable metrics like sales, transactions, employee turnover, guest feedback, keeping up with brand image, and repair/maintenance—helped earn us the coveted "Franchise of the Year" award at Burger King's 2003 global annual convention.

I HAVE NEVER FIRED ANYONE

In my career, I have never fired a single person. Yes, I even say that having managed hundreds of people and multiple stores at one time for decades. Why would I even want to fire someone? It was the last thing I ever wanted to do. As organizations, we spend vast amounts of time and money to locate and train talent. If I were to fire someone, I would have to start all over with someone else—this person could be even more ill-suited for the job.

Under my management, there was turnover; people left to pursue better opportunities, and people found the work unsatisfactory. More crucially, however, people "fired themselves" through their actions and inactions. As a manager, I had to tell myself that we didn't train our employees to come to work late, steal resources from our company, or not show up for work at all. The hard truth was that these actions were theirs. Similarly, we didn't coach employees to be unfriendly or keep their work areas dirty. These decisions happened, but they were made by the employees.

At one of our locations, we had a team member whose job was to greet guests at the drive-thru. They worked from 9 a.m. to 5 p.m. on weekdays (Monday to Friday), along with a shorter shift on Saturday. The core of their job involved greeting guests in a friendly tone of voice over the drive-thru speaker. One morning, at about 9:15 a.m., I pulled up to the drive-thru speaker. I often would spot-check all of our locations at various times of the week to verify that our restaurants were executing operations at the highest level while seeing if there were any immediate things I could assist with. Most importantly, I was looking for opportunities to catch our people doing something right.

This employee greeted me promptly—our goal was within three to five seconds—but they did so with a very lethargic and non-energized tone of voice. It was almost as if they didn't want to be there—a red flag for me. Our exchange went something like this:

"May I help you?"

I responded in the friendly, energetic, and happy tone of voice we wanted from our team members.

"Hi, there! It's Bruno." (I normally would not have identified myself because I didn't want the team to put on a "show" for me. I wanted them to think I was a real regular guest so I could get a real, accurate experience. I could use what I observed later for coaching opportunities or to catch my team members doing things right.)

They immediately knew they had messed up. Why? Because we had already coached them that they needed to greet each guest—especially guests in the morning—with a friendly, energetic, happy-to-see-you tone of voice. Team members manning the drive-thru are guests' first impressions of the Burger King brand from a local restaurant standpoint. In our initial training, we made sure all drive-thru employees were aware of the importance of their role. This employee had also been inconsistent with these standards, and their file specifically included notes about being disinterested while manning the drive-thru. The last thing we wanted to do was start over by hiring someone new. However, we cannot settle for substandard performance in the very competitive quick-service restaurant market.

Once they realized I was at the other end of the drive-thru speaker, the employee's tone quickly changed.

"Oh, hi, Bruno. Sorry, I just clocked in a few minutes ago, and I'm still a little tired," she blurted out. I wasn't happy.

"I'll pull around and come inside," I responded. I pulled into a parking spot, headed inside, and found the location's general manager (GM). I asked the GM how quickly we could get someone to cover this employee's station; I wanted to sit down with the employee and speak with her about her performance. I also wanted to involve the store's GM because this could also be a teaching or coaching opportunity for him. It was clear that she had not gotten the message through our previous attempts, and something definitive needed to be done.

Within the hour, we had someone else wearing the drive-thru headset, costing us more in labor than we had originally planned for the day. Regardless, I was willing to spend the money so I could sit down with the employee and the GM. The first thing I did was ask the employee if they knew why we were having this meeting. They responded, "I think so. Is it because I wasn't friendly enough when I greeted you this morning?"

"Yes, this is it. Since this is not the first time, we feel it is necessary to let you know our plan to fix this moving forward," I responded without getting angry.

I explained to them that I knew they needed a job and an income from that job. They weren't working with us solely because they thought we were great people and because they enjoyed the free food. They also worked for us because they have bills to pay. Genuinely speaking, I don't want to see them unemployed. As a leader and manager, I cared about all my employees, even the ones who didn't fit in with our culture. I knew they needed work, but I suspected my team wasn't the right place for them. They couldn't meet our standards, and we should not have to repeatedly lower our expectations to meet any employee's substandard performance. If I accepted inferior performance, I would be creating double standards between employees—a surefire recipe for discontent—and holding my whole team back.

However, in cases like this, I separated my opinions of the employee's performance and my opinions of the employee as a person. I told them, "Please start looking for alternate work. We'll be cutting down your hours and beginning to look for someone to take over your work. However, please put me down as a reference, and I will do all I can to find you work."

I even wanted to point at the nearby McDonald's and say, "Go apply there." In some sense, if this employee performed over there at the same level they performed here, they would be helping us more than if they worked here. They were surprised at my willingness to be their reference, but my logic is straightforward. This employee working with me isn't helping me, my business, or my team. I viewed this process as a business decision. We had an area that needed improvement, and something had to be done. In cases where that problem involves personnel, getting them into another job prevents them from hanging around after their time while also giving them and my business a fresh start.

It is also worth noting that I didn't fire this employee. I cut down their hours and gave them a choice—shape up or ship out. This tactic—showing employees kindness and a willingness to work with them, either within your organization or in their next job—generally works well. They either meet your standards and have confidence in you as a compassionate leader or continue to underperform and end up in a different position. This particular employee found another job within a month, and we hired someone new and trained them until we were confident they could meet our standards. Until the new employee was trained, I was willing to pay the employees I trusted overtime to provide the high levels of service our guests expect. This story illustrates that it often costs a business more money to pay someone who underperforms than to pay overtime to someone who will perform at the highest level. I cannot say for certain how many customers this particular employee might have turned away from our locations due to their sullen attitude, but it is likely that they cost us more revenue than the cost of paying a trusted employee a little extra in overtime.

The employer-employee relationship runs both ways, and leaders have a responsibility to treat their employees well. Employers treat their employees well by paying them fairly, training them adequately, being transparent with expectations, empowering them with the necessary resources, consistently holding everyone accountable, and recognizing and thanking them for their victories. However, when we talk about employees "firing themselves," we should recognize that the behaviors that lead to underperformance stem from the choices they make and don't make. If an employee can't or won't show passion or follow the proper procedures guests expect, they shouldn't be forced to do anything they don't want to do. I will not coach an employee who does not want to be coached. Employees don't want to be coached when they are not a good fit for the job.

I have three types of conversations with underperforming employees: coaching sessions, pre-firing conversations, and firing conversations. Coaching sessions involve recognizing an area of improvement, offering feedback and a rationale for the feedback, and working with the employee to develop a solution. These are completely harmless, and almost every employee of mine has been coached at some point or another. Pre-firing conversations, like the one I had with the drive-thru employee, involve recognizing the futility of previous coaching sessions, making a note of how the low standards are harming the organization, and mentioning how their current position might not be a good fit for them. I make sure to discuss how, if they do not improve their performance, they are firing themselves. Great managers and leaders must ensure employees know they are not looking for opportunities to fire team members. After all, I never wanted to see any of my former team members unemployed. I truly cared about my people. However, if things aren't working here for either the employee or the employer, it might be a good idea for the leader and the team member in question to work together to find another position that is a better fit.

Firing conversations happen when an employee has chosen to commit a serious action that is not allowed in any organization. Doing things like stealing, falsifying records, or not showing up for work without calling are actions that the employee chooses to make, but they will likely lead to immediate dismissal.

No leader enjoys firing their employees. In fact, both formal and informal polls suggest that letting an employee go is every manager's least favorite part of the job. Many managers are psychologically devastated when they have to let someone go. Some even go so far as to retain underperforming employees solely because they don't enjoy the task of firing them. However, if managers viewed the process of letting an employee go as "their actions fired them" instead of "I'm firing them, and I'm a terrible person," the act of letting someone go becomes a much easier task. After all, underperforming employees are also likely unsatisfied with their job as well and are underperforming due to a lack of passion. Firing an underperforming employee should never be the manager's fault.

LOVE WHAT YOU DO OR LEARN TO LOVE WHAT YOU DO

In the last chapter, we explored the idea that underperforming employees often fire themselves through their actions or inactions. However, even leaders and managers often have bosses, standards, and metrics to meet; even self-employed folks need to generate a sustainable income to support their needs. So, how can leaders—or any employee for that matter—best meet the requirements of their position and the overall strategic goals of their organization?

There are probably many answers to this question, but one of the most important things anyone can do to improve their job performance is—unsurprisingly—enjoy and feel satisfied with what they do. In other words, the single biggest thing we can do to be more successful at our jobs is like our jobs. We must love what we do in order to be passionate about it. We can see examples of this in our personal lives as well as our professional lives. Loveless relationships lack passion—both people involved can go through the motions, but they'll be far from happy.

The same is true with our work. Love and passion mark the difference between a job and a career. If someone truly loves what they are doing and can't think of anything else they'd rather be doing for work, they have found a career. On the other hand, if work is just a job to someone, there could be a lack of passion for that work. There are several reasons why lack of passion exists in a workplace. In some instances, it could be the work environment, culture, or management. However, in a lot of cases, a change in work culture might not be enough.

Questions like "would my job satisfaction improve if the culture was exactly how I wanted it?" or "do I know what I want?" can help an employee identify where sources of unhappiness might stem from. Unsatisfied employees with the answers to these questions have two options:

1) Find a different occupation to be passionate about
2) Learn to love what you are currently doing

During my career, I always chose option two. I never dreamed that I wanted to work in restaurants, despite loving Burger King as a kid and eating there as often as my parents would drive the ten miles to the closest one to where we lived. If I was doing what I really wanted to do, I would be a sports broadcaster, my dream job; as a huge Chicago sports fan, being the next Bulls, Blackhawks, Bears, Cubs, or White Sox play-by-play man or commentator would be amazing. I did go to broadcasting school thirty-three years ago, but I never finished my demo tape. I did not want to do anything except sports, and I was not interested in reading the news or being a DJ. Around this time, I had a wife and two kids, with a third one on the way, and I did not want to impact my family by taking a pay cut. This brings up an important and interesting point—we all have dreams, and many of them go unfulfilled because of life circumstances. My family was more important than my dreams of being a sports broadcaster. Although it was hard to let the dream go, I couldn't live my life unsustainably wondering, *What if?* or dreaming about life as a sports broadcaster. In addition to working my day job, I was able to feed my passion with some high school games, some even for my own alma mater. In 1993, I did the sports broadcast for a Chicago radio station and had a blast. In fact, I got the gig by winning a contest that involved faxing in the top ten reasons why I should be the sports commentator.

I use this story to reflect on the fact that I learned to love what I was currently doing. We can all do this in what we do. While it might not seem like a choice, everyone has the ability to find happiness in things around them. Of course, there are toxic situations that are unsustainable; however, there are millions of workers who could be happier at their jobs if they just committed to learning to love what they do. Sure, it might not be their dream career, but it's helping no one if you're miserable until the perfect opportunity comes along. Learning to love what we do is a much better choice than being unhappy, complaining, and constantly thinking about doing something else.

For us, our success comes down to the fact that all of us put our hearts into everything we did. If your heart and your employees' hearts are not in the work, you will only find moderate success—at best. To really take things to the next level, we have to be committed and passionate and love what we do. This becomes especially true when we are entrusted to lead others.

A GOOD EMPLOYEE IS NOT ALWAYS A GOOD MANAGER

It might seem intuitive that a good employee will naturally make a good manager. After all, they have certainly proven themselves in the tasks of their job, so wouldn't leading others to do the same come naturally to them?

Surprisingly, the best employees might not always make the best managers, and placing them in a supervisory role can be detrimental to them and the rest of their team. When making decisions on who to promote to a managerial role, an employee's ability to carry out their tasks should certainly play a role in the overall decision, but it shouldn't be the deciding factor. In the fast-food realm, a manager who doesn't know how to effectively prepare menu items or salt french fries will be ill-equipped to coach other employees on these skills.

Now, let's say you have two employees. One is the best french fry fryer in the world, and the other is an average french fry fryer. If their ability to lead and inspire those around them is equal, the better french fryer should be made manager. However, this might not always be the case. Let's say the world-renowned french fry fryer is unable to motivate team members from a leadership position, but the average french fry fryer can. In this case, who should be made manager? Likely, the person who can motivate and inspire team members should be prioritized over the team member with the superior skill at performing the task. However, many times, decision makers use job skill as the determining factor to decide who should be made manager, and this tactic can be prone to failure.

Why exactly is this problematic? Placing someone who is used to doing a job well into a leadership role forces them to take responsibility for the work of others. Individuals with adequate leadership skills can usually ensure high standards through others without any issue; however, some star players turned managers might simply—rather than working to inspire and motivate team members to meet high standards—try to do it all themselves, which leads to inefficiency. After all, a manager is not supposed to do all the work by themselves, and the transition from peer to manager is not easy. Promoting an unprepared employee will create a leader who is simply not ready to manage their former colleagues.

Promoted from within should not mean promoted to failure. Someone being promoted should be prepared thoroughly before being given command. For instance, it might be helpful to give a prospective manager example scenarios to see how they wrestle with them or observe them while they practice managing during a specific task or shift. Hopefully, with the right preparation, they will eventually settle into a management style that will allow for their success. Handing someone leadership without validating their ability to manage team members is not ideal. Just because someone is great at making sandwiches does not mean they will be great at leading and motivating others to do so.

For me, this happened once in my career. In 1988, we had just opened our fifth and sixth locations over the span of three months. My boss (who had hired me seven years earlier) was already overseeing our four locations. The plan was to open these two new locations in 1988 and promote me to oversee three stores. She would oversee the other three, and we would both be reporting directly to the owner.

However, as mentioned earlier in this chapter, just because someone is good at one position does not mean they will be good at leading and motivating others who have that same position. For me, being the top performing GM did not mean that I was guaranteed to be successful as a district manager (DM). Being a DM required that I no longer manage and lead one location. It meant that I was responsible for teaching, leading, and developing three other RMs to do exactly what I used to do. I was no longer in the same location leading and managing the same team. I now had to be able to get things done in three locations through different GMs and their teams without taking over.

I was lost. I did not know how to let go enough—not undermining the GM or their team—while leading three locations and taking responsibility for the daily happenings at each location. I was twenty-three years old, struggling with having a new boss, and very stressed out about what was happening. I didn't really know what to do about my increased stress and responsibility. We had new managers and team members doing different tasks and new levels of responsibilities. On top of that, we were growing by 33 percent in a matter of a few months.

I literally asked to go back to being a GM. I felt comfortable in that position. I knew what to do, was passionate about it, and had high levels of success. I was granted this request. In 1989, I went back to being an GM. I stayed there for four years until I was truly ready to be promoted again when the opportunity arrived. This time, I was more prepared, mature, and ready to handle the promotion.

For me, taking a step back at a critical point in my career was the best thing I could have done. It allowed me to gain two steps forward later when the opportunities presented themselves. I didn't want to be known as the DM who failed.

Again, promoting (or hiring) someone to be a supervisor just because they were good or even the best at their previous role(s) does not mean they will be successful in new management roles.

Developing and investing in more/new leaders should be a top priority for any company that plans to grow.

HOW TO COACH

There are a lot of managers who "tell"; there aren't a lot of managers who coach. Many managers don't realize the difference. Most employees don't mind being coached, but many are weary toward being told.

We all probably know of some famous coaches. They're called coaches, not "tellers." They didn't become great coaches by "telling" their teams what to do. Instead, they coached their teams. Professional sports don't have a "Tellers Hall of Fame," but there is a "Coaches Hall of Fame."

Coaching is harder than telling. It takes more time, and it is never a one-size-fits-all exercise. Your employees are different; they have different needs, opinions, ideas, and skills. Telling them the exact same thing isn't as helpful as meeting them where they are and getting them where they should be. Coaching is just that. It's understanding where current performance lies, explaining where performance needs to be, and then working with everyone involved to create a plan to get there.

There are many styles of coaching. However, some of the most successful coaching—successful meaning most likely to achieve the intended result—follows the praise, coach, praise (PCP) model. PCP coaching forces managers and leaders to find something to praise in someone's performance before coaching them on what they need to do better. Then, after coaching them, we praise or reassure them again. This final praise leaves the interaction on a positive note.

In our restaurants, we used this technique to ensure quality, service, cleanliness, and courtesy, as well as keep employee morale high. One thing we would often do is randomly order a various menu item, take it aside, and literally "dissect" it. Take our flagship product, the Whopper, for instance. We would take its temperature, weigh it, take it apart, examine the toasting of the bun, measure the condiment amounts and distribution, and even look at the order of how ingredients were served. (Interestingly, the order of how ingredients are placed on a sandwich dramatically affects its taste and the guest experience. Try eating a Whopper sandwich upside down sometime to experience this for yourself.) Each dissection gave us lots to work with and offered our managers an opportunity to practice their PCP coaching.

Feedback would look something like this: "The temperature was perfect—hot and fresh—nice work! One opportunity is condiment distribution: the ketchup, onions, and pickles are concentrated in the center of the sandwich. When the guest first bites into the sandwich, they might get a dry or plain experience. Then, when they get to the middle, they might get a mouthful of condiments and not enough flame-broiled beef. Let's remember that, even though we have to work fast, we never want to sacrifice quality for speed of service. Lastly, the weight was spot on. Keep it up!"

In this instance, we were able to get at the heart of the issue: the condiment distribution. However, we also let the employee know what they are doing well. Too often, managers only focus on what can be improved. Solely focusing on the negative makes the employee associate interactions with the manager as negative and decreases morale. Managers should be seen as bearers of both good and bad news. As humans, we enjoy being recognized for our work. Managers should applaud employees for doing things correctly.

The more we can use the PCP way of coaching without telling, the more motivated our teams will want to be. It's no secret that motivated teams are more likely to work toward being the best at something. My managers knew that, while we were not the biggest company nor performing rocket science or brain surgery, we should always strive to be the best at what we do.

Lastly, it is critical that when we praise, we are specific in our praise. Average feedback is "Jim, I thought you did a great job with your work." Great feedback is "Jim, we were really impressed with how you interacted with the guests. Your eye contact, sincere smile, and non-rushed approach was critical in helping all of us have a great shift. We especially liked how you handled the upset guest whose order was inaccurate. Thanks for all you do each day!"

LEADERS ARE "ON STAGE"

It's worth noting that, as leaders, we are being watched at all times. Employees look to us whether we want them to or not; we set examples to those around us. When I first became a restaurant manager, I realized that many of my employees were weary of me, and some might even have feared me. I used the following strategy to change this. Activities like this should not be done often because they can quickly lose effectiveness, but when strategically done, they can resonate for months afterward.

During a particularly light portion of the day, usually after a mealtime, I would be in my office. One time, I yelled, "Hey, Jim! When you have a minute, please come to the office," loud enough for everyone to hear. The immediate assumption was that Jim had done something wrong. When Jim got to the office, I asked him to shut the door. I could tell he was very nervous, and I'm sure the rest of the team outside was whispering to figure out what Jim did and what the punishment might be. In the office, I told Jim what an amazing job he did on the shift that day. I made sure my body language looked passionate because I knew that the team could see into the office. I'm sure everyone thought I was really tearing into Jim. However, he was pleasantly surprised to receive positive and sincere feedback from his manager. When he went back on shift, the team all asked him what happened. When they found out Jim was actually complimented and appreciated for his fine work, they were all very surprised.

They began looking at the office and the role of the manager in a completely different way. Being called back into the office was no longer an item of dread, and many were looking for ways to receive the type of feedback Jim did. I wasn't the scary manager anymore. I was someone who cared for them and appreciated the work they did. They looked at Jim and how he performed his job, trying to emulate his actions. Of course, I chose an employee who would be a good role model, and my entire team saw the improvement in his morale afterward.

Another example of being "on stage" is when I would arrive at one of my restaurants. Whenever I visited a restaurant, I would walk the property—or drive around it if it was really cold—to see if there was anything out of place. Maybe I could find some lights that had burned out, some litter or cigarette butts on the ground that needed sweeping up, or trash cans that required changing. If I could take care of something I saw, I would just do it. Our team members inside would watch me picking up litter or sweeping dust from the drive-thru. By doing this, I was setting the pace and the culture.

After completing my exterior survey, I would go inside. I would make notes in my head of how the front door glass looked, how clean the vestibule was, and how the point-of-purchase materials on the windows and glass doors looked. I would then go to the restrooms. Imagine if a guest sees a dirty restroom. What conclusions might they draw about the state of our kitchen? Interestingly, many guests who walk in and don't go straight to the front counter or order kiosk first go to the restroom.

After washing my hands and making mental notes about anything that needed to be addressed in the restrooms, I would continue my path by walking through the dining room. In addition to looking for ways to improve the cleanliness of our restaurants, I would interact with our guests, asking them, "How is your meal today?" or "May I take your tray?" (only if they appeared to be done eating). Many times, guests would look at me funny and say they could clean their own tray. I would always reply, "Of course you can, but you don't have to. I would be honored to do it for you." Lastly, I would go into the kitchen and say hello to everyone, specifically looking for opportunities to praise them or catch them doing a good job.

I knew our teams were watching me as I did this. Of course, having employees witness me at work was not the main reason I did all of this, but it did go a long way in cementing the culture I wanted within our organization. Believe me, even if our teams are not looking directly at us, they are watching our every move as much as they can—perhaps out of the corner of their eyes. They want to know what pace and examples we are setting. Leaders need to know they are role models for their employees. Because of this, I tried to set a high pace with high standards and expectations in the name of delivering an amazing guest experience. Leaders are always "on stage," and we must speak and act in mature, professional ways if we ever expect our teams to be this way.

Now, our teams may not be constantly staring at us or looking at us as leaders. But you can rest assured that they are watching us out of the corner of their eyes, making mental notes themselves to see if we leaders are practicing what we preach/coach. And, if we are not, they won't say anything most of the time. Inconsistency between what we say and how we act and carry ourselves will lead to more disgruntled, less motivated team members who care less about how they perform their individual tasks each day.

Our actions as leaders have a profound effect on the teams we are entrusted to lead. The question is this: what type of profound effect will it have?

BE THE EMPLOYER OF CHOICE

In every industry, there is probably an employer of choice. For one reason or another, candidates want to work there. The reasons might be tangible: company A provides better benefits or a higher salary, or the offices of company B are more modern and ergonomic. The reasons might also be intangible: company X has more prestige within the field, or company Y has better organizational culture.

Being the employer of choice has its benefits. When recruiting, you will likely attract the most applicants and the best, most qualified talent. Employees will take pride in the fact that they work for you and will likely be proud ambassadors of your brand to their friends and family. Despite these benefits, being the employer of choice is not always on managers' radars.

It should be a goal of every employer to be the employer of choice in their respective industry. But what exactly does being the employer of choice entail? I think we can most clearly see if we are an employer of choice based on how current and former employees describe working for us. Are they saying, "It was a great place to work. I learned a lot, had fun, and was treated with respect. My ideas matter and were welcomed. I would highly recommend anyone that is looking for work to try and get a job with them"? If they are a former employee, what are they saying about why they left? Was it related to the job itself or something else (moving to another city, going to school, or switching careers)? Finally, would they ever consider going back?

If your employees are answering these questions positively, it's likely you are well on the road to becoming the employer of choice. On the other hand, if your current and former employees are identifying specific areas where improvement is necessary, it might be worthwhile to devote resources to improving the employee experience.

Throughout my career, I saw several humbling examples that hint at the possibility that we were considered an employer of choice over the years. For example, we had college-aged employees returning to work during school breaks and telling us, "I look forward to coming back because I have fun working here." However, there's one story that makes me almost cry with pride.

I was driving to play basketball with a friend of mine and his son (a college junior at the time), and we got to talking. My friend's son—who is presently a lawyer—worked for us for about a year while in high school. He left on good terms because he got a job that was closer to his house. This meant he didn't have to head four miles across town to our Burger King.

Anyway, I asked him where he was working. He told me, and then he said, "Burger King was the best place I have ever worked at."

I said, "Nah, you're just saying that because I'm in the car." He shook his head. So, I asked, "Why is that?"

He replied, "Well, I was actually trained in how to do my job. Also, the schedules were posted in advance so I could see when I was supposed to work. And . . . it was fun."

Making a great work environment is not rocket science. It really is all about the simple things, like investing in proper training, ensuring schedules are posted in advance, and creating an atmosphere where people have fun while they work. As leaders, we must show that we truly care about the success of our employees and respect them as people with a life outside of their job.

WORDS AND DEFINITIONS MATTER

Every organization has a product and a target market for that product—no organization is perfectly circular. Every organization delivers something to someone else outside that organization. Of course, the specific deliverables vary from industry to industry: restaurants serve food, retailers sell specific products, and software companies sell digital capabilities.

In our restaurants, we did not give food to customers. We served meals to guests. This distinction between a customer and a guest might seem small, but it makes a big difference. How a business and its employees views their customers impacts the culture of the organization. Ultimately, it's a mindset thing.

Let's think, for a moment, about the difference between a customer and a guest. In the restaurant industry, customer service matters. When we define the recipients of our products as guests, we felt our team members consciously or unconsciously went into every interaction with a different mindset than if we called them customers. The word guest itself carries certain specific connotations, and we wanted our team members to feel that they are serving guests in their establishment as opposed to simply giving food to customers.

Another way we encouraged better performance through

definitions was by referring to our employees as team members. Our rationale behind this was very similar to why we called customers guests. We wanted our employees to feel valued and appreciated—like they were part of a team that depended on each member. They weren't just employees. They were members of a team.

Both of these definitions—although they seem like very small things—contributed to high levels of employee performance and satisfaction within our restaurants. They made employees feel valued and led many to take considerable pride in their work, simply because they saw themselves as team members and saw customers as guests. This has happened in many other industries. For instance, the term "flight attendant" has replaced "stewardess," and "server" is used instead of "waiter" at many restaurants.

I encourage every manager to take a look at the words used within their organization. Are words defined in the best possible way? Are things described in a way to maximize team satisfaction and performance? If not, how might words be changed?

STRESS THE WHY BEHIND EVERYTHING

Did you ever have a parent, teacher, or manager who, when asked why, would always respond *because I said so*? Or their actions and body language communicated a *"because I said so"* message?

If so, how did that make you feel? Were you frustrated and annoyed? Did you trust that person's leadership? Did you think they had your or your organization's best interests in mind?

Frustration and annoyance in situations like these are normal, if not expected. We want to know the "why" behind what we do, especially if we cannot easily see the end goal. Knowing the "why" behind an action can lead to team members feeling more motivated, as they can see the importance of their role in the larger picture. On the other hand, not knowing the why behind something can be harmful to employee performance and morale. Employees who don't understand the "why" behind their actions might view specific tasks as chores or not see the value in doing things a certain way. In other words, if they don't see the end product of their hard work or don't realize why things are done the way they are, they will not take as much pride in their work.

I want to emphasize that it's not the employee's responsibility to immediately see the "why" behind how things get done. It's on the manager to show their employees and teams the "whys" behind what they do. One of the best ways to demonstrate the "whys" is to explain the end result. Not always being punctual might not seem like a big deal to a specific employee. However, explaining to the entire team that one employee being late forces other employees to work extra hard and puts everyone behind might cause employees to better understand and appreciate the value of being punctual. After all, we didn't ask employees to be punctual simply because we wanted to make them suffer—there are reasons behind expectations. It's your job as the manager to explain them and justify why they are important to your employees.

For instance, I tried to instill the importance of showing up to work by emphasizing that we cannot effectively function as a team if we do not have enough members willing to contribute to the effort. It may seem intuitive, but I was surprised how effective reinforcing this principle really was. There are legitimate reasons when you should call off work; however, employees will be less likely to skip work if they understand the importance of being a part of the team. As an example, let's say five team members are scheduled for a shift and only four show up. The four team members now have to work 20 percent harder, be more efficient, and accept a higher workload. In many industries, being short-staffed leads to cut corners and work left behind. In the restaurant world, I've seen understaffing lead to decreased order accuracy, reduced quality, less clean restaurants, and a worsened guest experience—as you can imagine, rushed team members have less of an opportunity to be polite.

Here's an example of how being a few minutes late can affect the entire operation. We had a team member scheduled to work the front counter who was running a few minutes late. The person on the shift before couldn't stay, forcing the manager on duty to have to cover both the drive-thru and the front counter. During this, a large party came in and had questions about the menu and a new sandwich we had just rolled out. While the manager was giving his full attention to these guests, a car pulled up to the drive-thru. One of the main advantages of the drive-thru is speed and efficiency, and the guest in this car was clearly in a hurry. The manager—who was still in the middle of a conversation with the party at the counter—told the drive-thru guest that he'll be with him in a moment. We trained our team members to say this when we couldn't immediately take a drive-thru order. In this situation, saying this bought the manager about thirty seconds of additional time. Unfortunately, he still wasn't ready to take the order after thirty seconds.

This prompted the guest to yell in a frustrated tone into the speaker, "Hello, is anyone there?" Drive-thru guests are often in a hurry, and waiting thirty seconds can easily feel like an eternity. Like in most situations, perception is reality to most people.

The manager who was trying to cover both the drive-thru window and the front counter was feeling the stress of being short-staffed and responded again, "I'll be with you in a minute." However, this time, the guest could hear and "feel" the manager's frustration in his tone.

The guest then drove around to the window and started banging on the glass. When the manager went over, the guest started screaming and demanded to speak to someone "more important" than the GM for the location. The manager gave the guest my contact info, and I took it upon myself to personally try and make things right, which was not an easy task. The entire process took over an hour. I had to speak to the manager involved to get their side of the story and then call the guest back. All of this could have been avoided if one team member showed up for their shift a few minutes earlier.

I shared this story with team members to emphasize the importance of being on time for scheduled shifts. After hearing this, members of our team had a newfound appreciation for being on time. Simply reminding them that being a few minutes late can have major complications on the entire organization gave them a new perspective and taught me that everyone needs to truly understand the reason behind *why* they do something a certain way—even if it might be obvious for us.

COMMUNICATION IS THE OIL IN RELATIONSHIP ENGINES

Cars are phenomenal machinery, and to stay running, every engine requires oil to function properly. Without oil, an engine cannot run, and a car will not be able to drive. If a business was a car or an engine, communication would certainly be the oil that keeps that engine going.

Communication is found in all aspects of a business: employees communicate with each other, managers communicate with employees, and—perhaps, most importantly—employees and managers both communicate with customers and build relationships with clients.

If I had to choose between overcommunicating and under-communicating, I would choose overcommunicating. However, like with most things in management, there is an ideal balance between the two.

The danger with under-communicating is that it often involves making assumptions. When things are not explicitly said or explained, people have to make assumptions to fill in the gaps. I've seen countless individuals assume someone—employees, peers, supervisors, vendors, family, and friends—knows something when they did not, leading to miscommunications or misunderstandings.

Overcommunicating can also be dangerous. The recipient of our message might feel burdened by us or assume we think poorly of them because we are giving them information they already know.

For these reasons, we must create a balance. It's important for both parties to ask questions and get clarification on what's going on. If the message is not clear, important items get lost in translation, and mistakes happen. Do-overs can be costly to businesses' reputations, damage productivity, deflate morale, and lead to poor operations. This is why, as leaders/managers, we need to be approachable—whether in person, on the phone, or electronically. We must create an environment where our teams are comfortable communicating with us. Always keep in mind that being available to our team members is not the same as being approachable.

The game "telephone" is a great example of how lapses in communication can multiply as messages are passed down from person to person. In this game, people sit in a circle, and one person whispers something secretly to the person sitting next to them. The message is passed along from person to person until it travels the full way around the circle. Most times when this game is played, the message at the end is very different from the original message. This game shows people interpret messages differently, leave out key words, or hear things incorrectly.

Under-communicating occurs all the time throughout our lives. I try to overcommunicate because I have personally seen what happens when people under-communicate and let assumptions fill in uncertainties.

We were opening a new restaurant and getting things ready for our first guests to arrive. There were so many details to take care of in a very short period of time. For instance, we had to train a whole new team. For many, this was their first job. I asked one of them to stock the straw dispensers in the dining room. Back then, the straws that we used in the dining room were unwrapped, and our guests would dispense the straws themselves from little machines. However, the straws we used in the drive-thru were wrapped, as they were being handled by our drive-thru team members. I assumed the team member knew the difference between the two. When I went to check on how she was doing, I found her unwrapping the wrapped drive-thru straws one at a time and stacking them in the dispenser for the dining room. She had left quite a pile of straw wrappers on the table. All I could think to myself was *wow*. During this same time, I asked a different team member to stock a chilled drawer with milk cartons. I assumed they knew I meant to stack the individual cartons of milk in the drawer; however, I found them opening all the cartons and pouring the liquid milk into the drawer. These two lessons showed me what happens when under-communication takes place.

It is important to always keep in mind that communication is not a one-size-fits-all activity. When sending a message to an audience (this could be one person or millions), we must seek to understand our audience for the purpose of determining how much detail is needed for them to understand a request or task. We must always show patience, allow them to ask questions for clarification, and listen without distraction or interference. Be sure that when your receiver is asking a question, you do not look bored or make them feel that their question is stupid. Be sure to give them your undivided attention and fully explain the answer. Keep in mind that a better-informed individual—someone who knows what to do and the why behind something—will be more likely to perform a task correctly, leading to better performance.

Also, when questions that may seem "stupid" are not asked, "stupid" mistakes may happen. These can lead to wasted time, wasted products, or broken equipment. Worse yet, something much more serious might happen, like someone getting hurt.

There is never such a thing as a stupid question. When a person feels that a question they have asked is stupid, they may be less likely to ask questions in the future. If a manager repeatedly makes people feel bad about the questions they ask, the whole team will be less likely to ask for clarification. Imagine the threat to performance if your team is hesitant to ask for clarification. Not asking "stupid questions" can lead to stupid (and easily preventable) mistakes. The consequences from these mistakes are likely far worse than taking the time to answer what might be a "stupid question."

Lastly, whenever we receive a message, we need to confirm that we have heard and understood what is expected of us. If our conversation is face-to-face, this can be done with eye contact and a simple nod. However, since so much communication is done electronically these days, it is important that we acknowledge messages and let the sender know whether it was received (and hopefully understood). It is best to let the sender know we are on it, even if we can't fully respond until later.

Remember that an engine with no oil or bad oil will unquestionably break down!

WHERE TO LEAVE PROBLEMS (THE SUITCASE THEORY)

You've probably heard of people bringing their problems to work or bringing their problems home—this illustrates the concept of spillover. Spillover occurs when the stress of one domain affects a person's behavior in another domain. For instance, problems one evening can weigh heavily on the mind of a person during the next workday and affect their ability to do their job, or problems at work can affect a person's time with family. In both of these scenarios, spillover occurred.

I think it's helpful to think about work and home as suitcases. We all have two suitcases: one is for personal challenges, and one is for our work challenges. I coach employees to leave their personal-challenge suitcase outside the front door when they arrive for work. Don't worry, personal challenges are not going anywhere, and they will be waiting for us when we get off work. At work, we pick up our work suitcase. Our work time can actually be an escape from personal challenges, and when we leave work, we can simply switch suitcases.

People who bring their personal problems to work with them will struggle to concentrate because they are too distracted by other issues. The same can be said for the home as well; bringing work problems home prevents somebody from being fully present in the moment and unavailable to meet the emotional needs of family members. As people gain more experience and move into leadership roles within a company, it becomes more difficult to swap suitcases because managers become responsible for the actions of employees even when they are not around (in person). However, individuals should keep the suitcases separate whenever possible to dramatically improve both the quality of their work life and their home life.

Lastly, it is not fair for any of us to expect that others— including those we work with as teammates and those we live with (family, friends, etc.)—understand and accept our personal and work life challenges. This is especially true when our challenges affect their ability to get their jobs done. Alternatively, while on the home front, our unchecked challenges can lead to additional domestic, marital, or family challenges.

A good approach is to consciously take personal accountability, utilize the many resources available to us, and be proactive in managing our personal, mental, and physical health.

THE "BETTER JOB" MYTH

I've spoken to a lot of people who say they want a better job. I always ask them what they are looking for that would make it better. Many people—especially younger ones—will answer that they simply want more money.

I always tell people this: while more money or better benefits are legitimate reasons to start a job search, they should not be the only reasons. Surprisingly, research suggests money is not even listed as one of the top five reasons when people are asked to rate why they have chosen their current job or career. Even more telling are the reasons why people stay at a specific job longer. Money is rarely the number one reason why someone stays working where they are at.

Many times in my career, I volunteered to talk to teens and young adults who got in trouble with the law. Some were minor offenders (first-time petty theft), while others faced armed robbery or even felony theft charges—all of them had to listen to me as part of their "punishment." One place I frequented was the "boy's home" in my hometown, St. Charles, Illinois.

Let me tell you, these kids were hardcore. Even the pin on my name tag was considered a weapon, so I had to check it in at security. Once I was inside, I would role-play with them, coaching them on various management and workplace scenarios. I'd ask them this: "Imagine that you are working somewhere where you really like your supervisor(s), they value you and your work, and they treat you like you are an important part of their team. You generally and genuinely enjoy the work you perform each day. Your work schedule is good and fits well with your lifestyle. The travel is not too much, the pay is fair, and you get merit-based raises on regular intervals. Then you hear about a job through a friend that will offer more money than what you are currently making."

Many people would jump for the offer with more money, but there are a lot of things to consider that might not be immediately known. Let me challenge the new opportunity you've been presented with. Are you going to get the hours and schedule you need? In some organizations, as the new guy, you may have to work your way up to the schedule you would like. Often, being paid a higher hourly rate does not always result in higher pay because you're scheduled for fewer hours. Will you like the people you work with or the supervisor? They may have seemed nice during the interview, but there is a possibility that things may change once you begin. Thinking about the whole context, simply leaving a comfortable job for one with slightly higher pay doesn't make sense. Could there be a way to test out both jobs at the same time to prevent making a wrong decision? Then, if the new job is not all you thought it would be, you can still continue at your current one.

It is also worthwhile to consider why the "better job" might be hiring. They might be growing and have more roles to fill—this is a very legitimate reason to hire—but vacancies can also indicate an organization is struggling to retain people. Could it be that people who work there are unhappy? Is the work culture there unsustainable? Why might people be leaving that organization?

The students I worked with were often very receptive to what I had to say. Some of the students would go so far as to ask for jobs at my restaurants. Even the teachers would come up to me afterward and tell me that they had learned something. As a manager, explaining the better job myth to employees might help reduce turnover, and I believe anyone active in the workforce should keep the better job myth in mind when considering moving jobs to ensure that they are making the best possible decision.

CONSISTENCY SELLS

Let's imagine you are six hours into a long road trip. You're far from home and in a place you've never been before. It's lunchtime, and you need to grab a bite to eat. There are two restaurants to choose from. One is a local diner promising the "best burgers in town," and the other is a franchise of an internationally recognized restaurant brand. You could try the local diner and gamble on the quality of food and overall service. After all, it could be phenomenal or woefully disappointing.

Or you could do what millions of people do each day and visit the internationally recognized brand-name restaurant. Since the menu varies little from location to location, you know exactly what they serve there and what the food is like. You have a good sense of approximately how much the food costs and what the cleanliness of the place will be. One of the strongest factors behind the success of restaurant chains is the assured level of consistency at each location. This consistency builds trust among guests. Successful chains set high standards system-wide to ensure that the food being served to guests in rural Minnesota matches the food being served to guests in the heart of Manhattan.

With these restaurants, however, there isn't just consistency between locations. There is also an emphasis on consistency between days. The burger you order on Tuesday should taste just as good as the burger you order on Friday. This consistency makes these restaurants attractive options. It is human nature to want consistency—it gives us an anchor, and we seem to crave it in everything we do.

Because of this, lapses in consistency can have detrimental consequences to any business. A person can visit a restaurant ten times and receive a perfect experience nine out of those ten times—perfect food, great taste, warm ambience, prompt service, kind server, and good value. Numerically, a 90 percent satisfaction rate looks great on paper. However, the numbers don't tell the full story. What is the person likely to remember? Interestingly, they'll be more likely to remember the one time when things did not meet their expectations, and they might even put more weight on the negative experience when making decisions on what to eat in the future. What are they going to tell their friends and family? Will they be sure to emphasize that things are almost always perfect, or will they go into detail about how things went wrong on the tenth visit? As a business owner or manager, would you want to risk that?

Consistency is an often underappreciated aspect of running a business, especially one in the service industry. Guests want and crave a consistent experience, and the most successful restaurant brands have seemingly perfected this. Managers at all levels and within all industries should focus on driving consistency. Take some time to understand the perfect guest experience, and then tailor your management style to replicate this experience for everyone who walks through your doors.

Customers/clients prefer consistent companies over companies that perform amazingly one time and are a train wreck the next.

PEOPLE QUIT BOSSES, NOT JOBS

Job satisfaction is one of the most discussed and studied concepts in human resources. Low job satisfaction leads to low productivity, low morale, and, ultimately, high turnover and low retention. People who are not satisfied with their job seem to underperform until they've had enough.

As you can imagine, low job satisfaction is a lose-lose situation for all involved. Employees are not happy at work and put less effort into their duties. Managers will see underperformance and feel low morale among their teams and, in many cases, will become unhappy too. Clients and partners will begin to notice the decline in quality and service. Even worse, word might spread about how a company is a "bad place to work."

In addition to the actual work itself, a major component of job satisfaction is workplace experience. What a job environment is like is almost as important as whether a person likes the work that they do. And, of course, a huge component of one's experience at work is how their managers and supervisors treat them. I would go so far as to say that people quit bosses—perhaps more than they quit jobs.

Can you think of a good boss you had? What made them good? Now, think of a job you didn't like. What did you not like about the job? How much did your bosses' actions affect how you felt working there? How much happier would you have been if your bosses had done a better job?

As a manager, realizing that you hold so much responsibility in an employee's perception of their job can be humbling and invigorating. It has made me more aware of my actions as a leader and led me to work hard to ensure that my restaurants were great places to work. Managers are not only responsible for ensuring teams can further the organization's goals; they are also responsible for making the workplace a great place to be. How they lead, how they interact with team members, and how they communicate the needs of the organization determines how employees feel at work.

Remember, people often quit bosses, not jobs.

IN THE SKILL OF MANAGEMENT, FAILURE TO TRAIN IS TRAINING FOR FAILURE

One of the key points behind this book is that great leaders can be made with the right training. It's just like any other skill. We didn't hire anyone in our restaurants expecting that they knew how to flame-grill a burger, salt french fries, or use a point-of-sale system. But I've seen countless organizations put individuals into management roles without equipping them with the adequate training to be successful in that role. It was like they were expected to already know how to be a good manager. People don't seem to realize that management is a skill.

Similarly, training is an investment in that skill. We cannot expect new managers to be put directly in their position with no training. Untrained managers are more likely to fail. Worse yet, organizations punish the untrained manager when—in reality—the organization itself dropped the ball by not effectively training the manager.

In our restaurants, management training was a given. New managers did not run a shift until they had five to seven weeks of training. They got five weeks of training if they were promoted from within because they had knowledge about the various roles in the restaurant. New hires, on the other hand, got the full seven weeks.

The whole first two weeks were spent on learning all the stations in the kitchen and the various roles that the team members they would be leading perform. We wanted our new managers to have a good sense of how our restaurants were managed on a shift-by-shift basis. During this time, they also got a chance to "get their feet wet" with managing teams. They had opportunities to troubleshoot how they might handle various situations in a controlled environment with minimal negative consequences. Importantly, they could try out various management styles and see what worked and what didn't.

To an algorithm or a consultant with a profits-above-all-else mindset, this might seem like overkill and a waste of resources. While there was an additional expense associated with giving our new managers this opportunity to become comfortable with their role, we saved more money over the long run because our managers were more effective and more capable. By contrast, organizations that throw new managers into leadership positions without ensuring they are ready also see dramatically higher turnover. As new managers experience problems and do not have the tools to effectively deal with them, they get discouraged. They feel they do not have adequate support and are at risk of leaving the organization. On the other hand, we saw less turnover because our managers weren't set up to fail. And, when tough challenges came (they will invariably come), they were more ready to handle them.

Not enough companies and leaders recognize that management and leadership are important skills to invest in. Companies spend eye-wateringly large sums of money on training, but few actually dedicate any portion of this to leadership and management training. In the short run, it might seem more cost-effective to save money by skipping out on formal and organization-specific management training. However, this is a huge missed opportunity because bad leadership—as I'm sure you can imagine—costs companies a lot of money. Employees are unhappy and leave, customers and clients are unsatisfied and don't return, and the ability of the organization to do what it needs to do is impaired. The losses due to bad management dramatically outweigh how much leadership training and development costs. Leadership training is an investment that, when done properly and consistently, leads to less costs in overall labor and increases in top-line revenues. This is because the operational execution will be higher and more consistent. In other words, the organization will be run by highly motivated team members and led by effective managers who have been properly trained.

I encourage all leaders to consider how to incorporate management and leadership training into their training schedules and labor budgets. I also think individuals about to start in management roles should reflect on how their new job offers them the opportunity to learn, practice, and develop their management and leadership skills. If there isn't room to do so, they might be being set up to fail.

DON'T ASSIGN SOMETHING YOU'RE NOT WILLING TO DO

We've spent most of this book describing a key component of management as the ability to leverage the talents of those around you to achieve the goals of an organization. Having this ability is certainly a privilege and comes with perks. For instance, more work can be accomplished in a shorter amount of time. A single person could never cook enough meals to serve our regular guests and ensure safe and efficient operation of a restaurant.

As a manager, having the ability to utilize others might make someone think that they will no longer have to do certain undesirable or boring tasks because they have somehow earned the right to tell someone else to do it. I've seen many supervisors ask someone else to do a task simply because they do not want to do it themselves.

This is not good for morale. A manager assigning a task because they do not want to do it sends the message that the task itself is undesirable, and the employee assigned the task will not approach the task with a positive mindset. Employees look up to their managers and base their actions on their manager's actions and conform to the culture their manager has set.

Letting your teams know that you are willing to do whatever it takes to get the job done can be powerful. Building morale starts with showing your employees that you value the tasks you assign them, and avoiding the work they do or making it obvious that you are assigning duties because you would rather do something else accomplishes the opposite. Managers must show their employees that nothing is beneath them.

I've seen a lot of managers have the "it's not my job" mentality. Someone becomes a manager, and suddenly, they act as if their entire job has changed. They refuse to help out and give off an air of superiority, indicating that tasks they were recently performing are now beneath them and don't apply to them because "managers don't do that."

While we have discussed the importance of learning how to let go as a leader and that management is about learning how to lead and motivate to get things done with others, there will be times that we all still need to be willing to jump in and get our hands dirty with our teams. It can be done very strategically and have powerfully positive repercussions.

One day, after a midmorning corporate regional meeting (the type of meeting where many of us wore suits or sport coats at the very least) that ended at 2 p.m., I stopped by one of my locations just to say hello and try to catch our teams doing something right. I was there just before 3 p.m. Dishes were all over the place, and I could tell everyone was way behind. So, I decided to jump in and help. As I took my coat off and rolled up the long sleeves on my button-down shirt, a team member came in to work at 3 p.m.

She saw me starting to do the dishes and asked, "Why are *you* doing dishes?"

I replied, "Well, they need to be done. We have been a little busier today than we thought, and things need to get done." It turns out a nearby McDonald's had suffered a power outage from 10 a.m. to 1:30 p.m., so we had received many of their guests. Not long after that, she came back to start helping me. Although my dishwashing abilities weren't frequently called upon, we made quick work of the remaining dishes, and the restaurant was back on track within forty-five minutes. I even showed her a few tricks I had learned a few years earlier, including that dumping out lettuce and juices into a garbage can first maximizes the longevity of the dishwater. Most importantly, we had fun, and I showed the team that I am willing to get down and dirty. If I can do it, they should truly never have an excuse to not get them done as well.

Believe me, I understood that me taking unexpected time out of my day to help coach and lead my team around this task would resonate throughout my locations. I hoped my managers would see me contributing to the frontline operations and internalize that they should be prepared to be teammates and help however they can. I'm sure the sight of me in a suit doing dishes got around our stores. I said this before: our actions as leaders are powerful. We are on stage at all times.

A lot of times, the "it's not my job" mentality stems from someone disliking specific tasks. We need to tell ourselves that it's okay to not like everything about our jobs. We can have coworkers we wouldn't invite for dinner, and we can have duties that we'd rather not do. No job will always be perfect. The definition of the word *job* doesn't involve zero stress and coworkers who are always fun and lovely. I'm sure even the travel bloggers who get paid to hop from beach resort to beach resort occasionally have something to moan about. My point is that every job has aspects that are not always going to be enjoyable, and that's to be expected.

In the restaurant business, there are necessary tasks that some people might not want to do—for example, doing the dishes, mopping floors, cleaning the kitchen, and working late nights, holidays, or weekends. Even though we might not want to perform these tasks, we should always respect what everyone does as part of their job. Respecting employees' responsibilities helps build and maintain morale. If you cannot respect a task and be willing to do it yourself, you might be better off in a different line of work.

Respecting the duties of your team involves thanking them sincerely. Your team likely thrives on positive feedback and appreciation. However, everything is probably not always praiseworthy, so constructive feedback is likely needed every so often. As we've discussed elsewhere, constructive criticism is about delivering the "bad" in a way that still makes people feel good about themselves and proud of the work they do.

I like to frame points of constructive criticism as opportunities, and I especially like to structure the whole conversation around us being a team. I (the manager) am not against you (the employee), but I want to help you succeed and achieve the organization's goals most effectively.

Our employees need this type of genuine, positive, and appreciative feedback especially after a particularly stressful time. They rallied. They need to be recognized. My rule (like many) is, praise in public, counsel in private. And, even when I'm counseling an employee, I start from the good and build from that position. The occasional times I need to counsel in public, I try to make it a positive experience for all parties. As I mentioned earlier in the book (it's so important that it's worth mentioning again), I've learned that people don't like to be "told" what to do, but they usually don't mind being coached on what to do. Average leaders tell people what to do. Great leaders teach and coach people.

PARTNER WITH YOUR PARTNERS

Every business—regardless of size or industry—interacts and manages various supporting vendors. The biggest brands in the world were built on the shoulders of successful relationships with vendors and industry partners. A single business can't do it all, and any manager who thinks they can do it all is setting themselves up for failure.

Vendors supported us by supplying goods and services, repairing and maintaining equipment, and helping us serve our guests. They were integral parts of our business model, whether they knew it or not. Our vendors were true partners. They knew that their success was predicated on our success. In many ways, we didn't pay our vendors; the guests eating our flame-grilled Whopper sandwiches, ordering at the drive-thru, and filling their drinks at the soda fountain were the ones paying our vendors' invoices.

Our vendors' responsibilities involved enhancing our team's ability to serve our guests. This meant they effectively had two customer bases—our internal teams were the direct recipients of our vendors' services, while our guests were indirect recipients. If our vendors underperformed, our teams underperformed, and our guests were more likely to be unsatisfied.

Take an HVAC unit on the roof of one of our restaurants as an example. Each HVAC unit had an access panel with six large screws. Just looking at an HVAC unit required all six screws to come out of the access panel. If a screw was left on the roof and someone stepped on it, the screw could easily puncture the roof, and the location would have to deal with a leaky roof and stained ceiling tiles—not to mention our guests having a poor image of our brand and the time and money involved with fixing or replacing the roof. In other words, our vendors had a lot of power and influence on our ability to provide an amazing experience to our guests.

Because of this, I realized I had to team up with our partners to ensure everyone's best interests were met. Obviously, I don't want to micromanage our vendors, but I want to guarantee that they have our priorities on their radar.

One time, I pulled into the parking lot of one of our locations at noon—the busy lunch rush. I saw the truck that collects our used cooking oil from our restaurant storage unit parked near the exit of the drive-thru lane. The first concern I had was the timing of his arrival, but I decided to let the service tech finish before sharing my concerns with him since the hose was already connected. When he was done, I noticed a blob of grease on the wall below where he connected his hose to our newly remodeled restaurant. Every guest who left the drive-thru could possibly see this unappetizing blob stuck to the side of our restaurant.

I then approached the tech and started the conversation by saying, "Thanks for what you do. You were in and out very quickly, and we appreciate that. I will be calling our rep to discuss the timing of your service. We need to avoid having service trucks on our lot during busy lunch periods."

I then took him to see the grease blob, saying, "This grease blob doesn't look great on our newly remodeled restaurant, and every customer who pulls through the drive-thru might see this and lose their appetite when they are about to eat the food they just purchased." I asked him, "Do you have anything on your truck to clean this with? Maybe a towel and degreaser?" He shook his head no. So I took him into the restaurant and grabbed a towel and what we called "pink cleaner"—I wanted our team members to call degreaser "pink cleaner" because our guests shouldn't hear us say "degreaser." I felt it was very unappetizing to eat food in a restaurant and hear team members refer to something as a "degreaser." Before he left, I asked him what it would take to have these two items on his truck in the future in case a similar situation came up. He said it wouldn't be a problem.

I then called our sales rep to discuss the entire situation with him. I offered to come to their next team meeting, buy everyone pizza, and explain why what they do is such an important part of the success of our business. I would be able to discuss what it means to be a "vendor partner" and show them how we're all in this together.

A couple weeks later, I drove to their shop to attend one of their meetings, and their teams loved it. I told them that we chose them because they had the cleanest trucks and could best meet our schedule, even though competitors offered better rates. Of course, they liked the pizza, but I think they appreciated learning about the important role they played in our success. The same technician who serviced our restaurant a few weeks before was there and pulled me aside to show me his spotless truck that, of course, had a towel and degreaser.

THE IMPORTANCE OF PASSION

In my career, I've learned passion and motivation go hand in hand. Motivated employees are likely to be passionate about their work, and employees who lack passion probably lack motivation. As leaders, we show passion by teaching and coaching our teams about how and why our work is worthwhile.

Passion is important and *must* be shown through actions, not just words. In my experience, passion is the number one thing that leads to success at a high level—no matter what you're doing, period. The importance of passion can be seen in everything from your career to your relationships with those around you.

People who are at the highest levels of what they do ooze passion. The best in any field—be it sports, music, teaching, acting, writing, medicine, politics, broadcasting, etc.—are extremely passionate about what they do. Additionally, they know how to channel their passion into a focused work ethic that many others simply are not willing to match. This is what makes them stand out among the rest and keeps them committed to themselves and their teammates, and it's what got them to where they are.

Some highly successful people who are respected in multiple fields can apply their passion from one domain to another. Bob

Uecker was a Major League Baseball catcher; he was good but not Hall of Fame–worthy (of course, one has to be passionate about what they are doing to even make it to the major leagues). However, he took his passion for baseball and transferred it to broadcasting; he has been the lead broadcaster for the Milwaukee Brewers for the last fifty years. He eventually did make it to the baseball hall of fame, except he was inducted as a broadcaster. He also used his passion to launch a successful television career. He was a favorite guest on Johnny Carson's era of *The Tonight Show*, served as a spokesperson for Miller Lite, and landed a 122-episode run on a major sitcom (*Mr. Belvedere*). He even made it onto the big screen, playing Harry Doyle in the movie *Major League* and its sequel, *Major League II*. That's what I call transferring passion!

Many people think passion is like a light switch that gets turned on once we reach a certain income level or rank in the corporate ladder. However, this couldn't be further from the truth.

One day, I walked into one of my restaurants during the peak of a busy lunchtime rush. I immediately noticed a guest at the drive-thru window, looking upset and stressed out. It seemed like she was trying to get the attention of someone within the restaurant. I glanced around through the kitchen. Everyone looked very busy, so I went over to the guest and asked how I could help. The issue was small, and I could easily take care of it. Best of all, she left happy and satisfied. I sensed that service standards could slip during the rush, so I jumped into action and worked in the kitchen. I offered positive coaching and compliments to my team, and we were able to tackle the lunch rush.

Once things had settled down, the manager on duty asked me, "How can you be so nice to everyone all the time?"

I replied, "Why not? After all, the guests pay our paychecks, and our team members are our most valuable resource. It's bad business to not be nice to everyone."

The manager said, "Well, I suppose I could be nice too if I got paid what you got paid." This took me by surprise, and I tried to remain calm and professional.

I replied, "If you truly believe that, you will never make the money I make. Do you think passion is a light switch that you can turn on and off only after you make a certain amount of money?"

Working in a dream job or driving a dream car often requires us to pay our dues and gain experience. Everyone's road is different, and while we are on that road, we must exhibit passion for what we are doing. In the best case, the right person will notice our passion and give us a chance.

Now, some of you might be thinking that all highly successful people must like what they do. And you would be correct. As long as we are on this planet, we are all entitled to wake up each day. However, whatever we do between periods of rest is up to us. What matters most is what we are doing now and what we will do in the future. For instance, did the diners eating in our restaurants really care about any and all of the successes over the years, from operational awards to guests and team members who have expressed their gratitude for the experience they had in dining with us and working with us or all the KPIs that were met or exceeded and all the sales and profits that I was responsible for attaining? Should they care? I expect that all they care about is what is happening right now. Successful people know this and thrive on it. That's why I often tell people, "I have ketchup in my blood." Nothing else sums up my passion for what my career has been about.

As a manager, the question becomes this: can you transfer your passion to others so they will follow your lead? In the restaurant world, it was about getting everyone excited about serving hot, crispy, salty french fries, ensuring sparkling clean and fresh-smelling restrooms, and just about everything in between, more so than they ever thought possible when they applied for the job or accepted the position. As an aside, notice the descriptive terms that I have used in the previous sentence—I specifically chose those words because they show how passionate I am about these things. They were not just french fries or restrooms. I wanted my teams to know that I wanted hot, crispy, salty french fries and sparkling clean and fresh-smelling restrooms.

This passion translated into high standards and expectations. No matter what anyone is doing for their chosen career, they want to be part of a winning team. Winning teams are led by passionate leaders. Being passionate is not always the easiest thing, and it does not come naturally to many people. However, to be successful at the highest level in anything we choose to do in life, we must either love what we do or learn to love what we do. When we love what we do, we will be passionate about our work. If you are a leader who demonstrates passion and expresses excitement in your everyday work, you will find followers who will get excited. You will transfer your passion to them. Being a passionate leader or manager is about being a positive role model and always communicating your passion through your actions. Keep in mind that not all your followers will be willing participants. Some may need a different approach—this could be as simple as some private teaching and coaching. It could also require that we work together to find them a different role on the team (if possible) or—as a last resort—a different job on another team. We don't want people on our team who don't want to be there.

The more passion you can instill around you, the better chance that your teams will be passionate about their work, which will lead to your business thriving.

BEING A PROBLEM SOLVER VERSUS A PROBLEM IDENTIFIER

In business and management, not many things are certain. However, one thing that is certain is that problems will arise, no matter what industry you work in. In the fast-food business, a grill might break and need repairs, a menu item might not perform as anticipated, or the arrival of new competition might reduce daily traffic. It could be argued that the true test of a manager is how they react when a team they supervise—or their entire organization—is faced with a problem.

How managers tend to react can largely fall into one of two camps: problem identifying and problem-solving. Problem identifying and problem-solving both start very similarly: the manager recognizes there's a problem. But that's where the similarities end. Problem identifiers are excellent at calling attention to the existence of problems. These are the shift leaders who walk around the kitchen, noticing and mentioning every single protocol violation. However, they rarely offer suggestions to the employees on how to improve. Many don't even act like they want the employee to succeed. It seems like all they want to do is catch an error or find something broken.

Problem identifiers are a dime a dozen. It's easy to point out problems and find faults. Problem solvers can be tough to find.

Knowing that there's a difference between problem identifying and actual problem-solving is a powerful tool for managers. Most problem identifiers may not even know they are problem identifiers. Recognizing there's a difference allows a manager to stop and think about which type they fit into.

If the stakes are relatively low and a learning opportunity presents itself, great problem-solving managers might consider not immediately revealing solutions to a problem. The benefits to this are two-fold. If the employee and the manager arrive at the same conclusion, the employee will have had an opportunity to test and refine their problem-solving skills. But it's also possible that the employee might give a different answer—one that the manager didn't even consider. In any industry, a plurality of new and helpful ideas is always a good thing. Products, product lines, and even entire companies have been founded on the basis of new ideas.

Of course, problem-solving can go too far. Managers might micromanage, offering an unhelpful amount of suggestions on how to solve problems before an employee has had a chance to think about the situation. Similarly, managers who are too quick to propose their solutions might stifle innovation and reduce the likelihood that employees will speak up and offer their input. It's certainly possible that employees might have arrived at unique solutions but won't share their ideas if the manager has already spoken. Letting your employees have the first word in these situations is long-term planning. Two minds are better than one, and the frontline employees are likely closer to the actual situation itself. Even if you might have more overall experience, they might be the experts in this particular situation.

I've seen some leaders be afraid of seeking input from their teams because they fear they may no longer be needed. The train of thought goes something like this: If my employees are the ones thinking of solutions to their challenges, what role do I have? Doing this, however, inhibits growth and holds the team back because effective solutions from the frontline can't come to light and employees will be unable to think on their feet if their manager is not around. Second, learning the types of solutions your team suggests might help you better identify who might make good future leaders. Whenever I moved upward into different roles, I usually had the strongest voice in naming my replacement. How my team members did in problem-solving opportunities proved instrumental in helping me determine who I nominated. In these situations, I would see who is causing others to gravitate toward them and who is naturally able to serve as a leader by gaining the respect and trust of those around them. Great leaders are made, not born. As a manager, you can't expect your employees to be leaders unless you give them opportunities to lead.

The proof of empowered frontline leadership happens when the official leader is not around. What happens when the boss is on vacation or has a scheduled day off? Are things running like a well-oiled machine, or are there inconsistencies? Do employees feel comfortable being a part of their own problem-solving? If things slip noticeably, there probably isn't a culture of employee empowerment. If the manager/leader must be around all the time to ensure things are going well, then highly motivated, self-sufficient teams are not being developed. The official managers and leaders set that culture, and the employees—especially the ones with the potential to be future leaders—will respond accordingly. And, when things do need to involve you, will you be a problem identifier or a problem solver?

THE IMPORTANCE OF BEING HUMBLE

One of the most humbling and rewarding things that happened to me during my career was when I would walk into one of our Burger King restaurants and notice a new face behind the counter. We had the honor of having someone new join our team—how exciting!

Whenever I saw a new face, I would greet them by name, welcome them to our organization, and tell them I was happy they were on our team. To me, the first impression I made on them was more important than the first impression they made on me. I wanted our team members to feel special because I genuinely believed they were special.

Sometimes, I would hear that the new team member had heard of me and my way of doing things. I wanted to have some fun while being as humble as possible, so I would say, "Don't believe a word you heard about me. I'm sure it's not true." It was humbling to know that my leadership style had percolated up and down the entire organizational chart, and new team members knew who I was.

One of the worst things a manager or leader can do is be inconsistent between their words and their actions. I've met dozens of managers who say one thing but do something completely different, such as conveying an "it's not my job" attitude toward cleanliness needs and guest interactions. Employees will rarely point out leadership inconsistencies, and frankly, it shouldn't be their responsibility. If they do, however, we should be thrilled and never defensive. After all, they had the guts to risk retribution or retaliation to bring something to our attention. That deserves celebration.

The bottom line is that our words matter, but—more importantly—our body language, tone, facial expressions, and behavior matter much, much more. Leaders who do not understand this and do not take full advantage of the face time they get with their teams will be more likely to have employees who feel underappreciated. The idea of being an active presence with employees has never been more critical than now. We live in an age where so much communication takes place electronically. Because of this, when the opportunity to have face-to-face time with our teams arises, it is critical that we as leaders/managers take full advantage by focusing on what our team members are saying verbally and nonverbally (i.e., body language). Furthermore, it is important to follow up on actionable takeaways in a timely manner; otherwise, there is a risk of becoming someone who overpromises and under-delivers. Managers who cannot be an active presence with their employees risk creating an unproductive or frustrating organizational culture.

For many reasons, our restaurants performed better than their peers, and we were asked to serve the Burger King brand beyond just our walls. For instance, we became a training franchisee. This meant that other operators would be brought to our restaurants to witness new product launches and improved operational initiatives. We worked on behalf of all franchises in the region to negotiate contracts with suppliers and distribution and share our operational tactics with other restaurants in the system. These were honors that only the "best of the best" were invited to. Our team members were frequently invited to Burger King's corporate headquarters or other locations to test possible products, new equipment, and new procedures. We helped with marketing and governmental affairs for the brand—each year, some of us would go to Washington DC and discuss how proposed legislation would affect the restaurant industry. In these roles, I represented us and many other franchises. It was an honor, and I was proud to serve in this role.

Because of this, I had the opportunity to learn from some of the best leaders around and participate in case study analyses of some of the leading brands in the world. I learned how they sourced, trained, and developed their teams, as well as how they perfected organizational culture. These are the companies that can deliver amazing experiences and outcomes to clients on a consistent basis.

Take Ritz-Carlton as an example. Their culture revolves around the idea of "ladies and gentlemen serving ladies and gentlemen." If you ask a staff member at a Ritz-Carlton property where something is, they take you to it. They don't tell you how to get somewhere or point in a direction. Instead, they will walk with you and ensure that you get where you need to go. It is their perfection of the little details that make them one of the most imposing hospitality brands in the world. Of course, booking a room at a Ritz-Carlton is going to be more expensive than most other hotel brands, but enough people see value in the brand and are willing to pay for their level of attention to detail.

Harley-Davidson is another great example. This brand went from being the number one motorcycle company in the world to the verge of bankruptcy, but they were able to resurrect their brand and reclaim their spot at the top. And, last but not least, Disney is one of the best examples of a business manifesting success from their organizational culture. Disney calls their employees "cast members." They don't clock in—they "go on stage." When Disney employees are at work, they aren't working—they are "performing."

Every time I was at a leadership conference learning about how a brand was empowering their people, I took copious notes. I must have looked like a dork, but I wanted our whole team to get this information.

There's humility in recognizing that you can learn something from any successful business, regardless of what industry they might be in. I applied what I learned about organizational culture within Ritz-Carlton, Harley-Davidson, and Disney to our own operations. I asked myself and our teams, "How can we use this info and improve how we serve burgers and fries?" Our teams learned these concepts, and our entire organization became better able to unleash the power within our people.

GUEST RECOVERY

I'm sure a lot of managers dread having to deal with a guest that is unsatisfied, unhappy, or upset with an aspect of their experience. In these moments, tempers can flare, things can get heated, and it can spark a stressful situation for the manager.

However, rather than thinking about dealing with upset customers as burdening, why not look at the experience in a positive light? Here's why. When a customer lets us know about their negative experience by complaining, they're actually doing us a huge favor. Why? Because we can have insight on how to improve our service and product, and we also have the opportunity to go above and beyond a normal customer interaction. Dissatisfied customers who become satisfied by our recovery may actually become more loyal than a typical customer because they have had a chance to see us acknowledge and rectify our mistake. Plus, the customer will now get a chance to see what we are *really* made of; they will get a chance to "feel" how much we truly care about them as an individual.

Additionally, having customers leave dissatisfied is a tremendous liability for any business, considering that it is much more expensive to recruit a new customer than keep a current one. Creating a culture where employees are committed to continuously improving customer satisfaction simply makes good business sense. Studies show that customers are much more likely to talk about an experience they were dissatisfied with than an experience they were satisfied with. In today's world, negative experiences can go viral quickly, so it is more critical than ever for businesses to have a solid customer recovery workflow.

Let's say a customer comes to our restaurant five times. Four out of those five times, they are completely satisfied. On the fifth visit, something goes wrong, and they become unhappy. Are they going to tell their friends and family members—who might be current or potential future customers—that their experience was great 80 percent of the time, but one little thing could be improved on the last visit? Or are they going to focus exclusively on the final visit and use details to describe what went wrong? More likely, the latter, of course. Dissatisfied customers are much more likely to talk about negative experiences than positive experiences with friends and family. Thus, having individuals walking around with bad feelings toward your brand is not good for business. So, when someone tells you or a member of your team that things didn't meet their expectations, they're doing you a huge favor, and you have the rare opportunity to make them happy. Why? Because most unhappy guests don't give us this opportunity and instead quietly decide to take their business elsewhere.

Let's revisit the example. Let's say the customer came up to us on the fifth visit and let us know something went wrong. We listened to their concerns, gave them an opportunity to express their perspective and vent their frustrations, determined how we could rectify the situation, and made them satisfied in the end. Now, they're not going to tell their friends and family—current or future customers—about how things didn't meet expectations. Instead, they're going to talk about how things didn't go well, but the employees took a genuine interest in making things right. Right there, you've turned what would have become a liability on your brand into a strong asset.

But how exactly does one practice guest recovery? The first step is to listen—truly listen to the complaint and show empathy. This isn't the time to argue. Your guest is entitled to their feelings and their perspective on what happened. And, please, never take these kinds of situations personally. Most likely, the guest does not even know you on a personal basis; you are just the person on your team that gets to represent your brand to this guest. I've seen unbelievably frustrated and irate customers become polite when they feel truly listened to. I would often say, "I don't blame you for being upset. I would be as upset as you are. You have every right to be mad, and I truly understand." This diffuses the situation, especially when customers expect the person they're speaking with to get defensive, make excuses, or try to match their energy. This isn't the time to get upset; consider yourself the lucky one because you get a chance to try and recover the situation.

Early in my career, I realized how powerful my actions were in leading my team to view guest recovery in a positive way. From my office, I noticed a team member discussing something with a guest. I could see that things were taking longer than normal, so I headed over there to see what was going on and if I could possibly help. The customer was an older gentleman, and he was telling our team member that we had served his order cold. He smelled of alcohol and looked disheveled. I quickly surmised—along with the team members who were trying to help him—that he was trying to scam us for some free food. The team members had followed all procedures appropriately and explained that we couldn't do anything if the customer didn't have a receipt. The customer stated that he had thrown everything away since it was cold, and he didn't have the receipt. By this point, me and my team knew he was lying and was simply trying to get some free food from us. I could also tell that he wasn't going to leave without getting something, so I explained to him that we'd replace his entire order and give him some extra french fries for his inconvenience. I also took the time to explain why we require a receipt.

I said to him, "I know this is hard to believe because I'm sure *you* would never do this, but there are actually some guests who sometimes try to scam us for free food. Can *you* believe this?" I then gave him his order, which included those additional hot, crispy, and salty french fries I promised, thanked him for coming back, and made sure that he knew he was welcome back the next time he was in the area *and had a few dollars to spend.*

Our team was aghast. They were convinced he was scamming us. So why would we give him free food? I explained to them that, yes, he was scamming us, but he knew that we knew he was scamming us, and he wouldn't come back ever again, unless he had money to pay for his food. This turned out to be true, as I would see him hanging around other nearby businesses in the subsequent weeks and months, soliciting people for money and handouts. However, he was rarely in our restaurant again, and the couple times he was, he had money to pay for his food.

The bigger point here is that it may be better to lose a few dollars in food than risk interrogating honest, paying customers and creating a bad name for ourselves. Also, in this specific situation, I felt it was best not to argue with this guest and to get him out of the restaurant ASAP. In other words, I specifically didn't want the actions of a few to determine how we handle our day-to-day operations with the majority. We don't want our team members assuming the next guest who comes in with a complaint and no receipt is trying to scam them. Almost all our customers are good, honest people who are not looking to scam us for free food.

One time, a family called to let us know that we had forgotten to include one of the sandwiches they ordered. The caller was about to have Saturday night dinner with his kids at home and was upset that we had forgotten to include his sandwich. The normal procedure involves us writing down the error in a log to process a refund and possibly mailing out coupons to that guest or having the guest come back to the restaurant at their earliest convenience to pick up their missing item. However, I didn't feel like either of those would really do enough for this guest—after all, they chose to have Saturday night dinner with our food at home, and I felt honored to be entrusted with that responsibility. Not to mention, he was home alone with his kids, and it would have required him to pack up the kids again to come all the way back to our restaurant to get his missing sandwich. I wasn't going to let them down. I asked how far he lived from the store, and he said he lived a few minutes away. I asked him for his address, and then I told him I'd be on my way with the sandwich, some extra fries, and some desert. He sounded surprised and made sure I was really willing to do this. It was my pleasure, and I dropped off the food. This customer's entire family became some of our most loyal guests, and they likely told all their friends about the time the restaurant went above and beyond.

Later on in my career, when I was further away from the day-to-day operations of a restaurant, I would only get to deal with the angriest customers. These were the ones who were so mad that they wanted to talk to someone "important" up the management food chain. In these situations, I employed the same principles with success. I listened to their complaints, tried very hard to see their perspective, acknowledged their feelings, and worked with them to find a solution for both of us. Importantly, I learned that leaders create a culture around emphasizing service recovery. Doing so leads to more loyal guests, team empowerment, and better sales.

CONFIRMING IT ALL

Many of us who read leadership writings and management articles or books wonder if the things we read can really make a positive difference in our careers and lives. On paper, they sound great—if not too good to be true—most of the time.

There are—and always will be—many ways to measure true success. To some, success is money, profit, fame, or status. To others, it might be about helping others, sacrificing for them, and serving them. But does it have to be either-or? Can serving others be profitable?

I've spoken to hundreds of people in my career who want balance. We all want balance. Heck, if we aren't physically balanced, we fall down. Let's take a closer look at what balance might mean for different people.

I believe the person leading any risky or challenging adventure—whether that's a business or a sports team—should stand to gain the most. Take a large business and its founder. That person might have been responsible for creating tens of thousands of job opportunities. This means leaders also have the unique opportunity to serve others. The more and better we do that, the more success those people will have in their lives as well. Whether they make a career out of it (as I did) or take the experience into other areas of their life, truly serving others can be so profitable.

Balance, in my life, means allowing others more opportunities to live the life they choose while learning to embrace and appreciate the simple, little things more often. I often wish we had a way to find out what every person who ever received a paycheck from us is up to now. I know many who are doing very well and seem happy overall.

These days, I see and read a lot, especially over the last couple of years as I plan the next stage in my career. I see job descriptions frequently use terms like "culture builder" or "willing to embrace and leverage a collaborative work environment"—this makes me think that so many organizations are embracing the idea that leaders should be people developers. The fact that people development is so central to their job descriptions is a very good sign. Put another way, companies are looking for "leaders," and those leaders need to have solid, soft skills and be supremely good people developers.

This is, of course, very encouraging. However, the big challenge is putting these ideas into practice. I discussed earlier that one of the most damaging things an organization can do is say one thing and do another. In management, this looks like saying all the right things about leadership and management philosophy—the buzzwords found in all the major business books—but doing something else. I've read enough performance reviews and connected with enough people to realize that this disconnect happens far too often. In my experience, this happens often because managers and leaders have not been taught to properly lead. However, there's a silver lining here: great leaders <u>can</u> be made.

I will end for now with a story that happened very recently. It demonstrates how using the principles and strategies discussed in this book will make a difference in your life and career, as well as the life and career of those you serve.

My wife and I were recently returning from our annual Tour de Florida—a ten-day whirlwind trip across the state to see family and friends—when I got a random friend request from one of our former managers. I had not seen nor spoken to her in more than nine years. She had started with us part-time while in high school and remained with us for just over ten years. She never directly worked for me, but we knew each other. She became a very good manager and was happy in that position. I saw her often in the restaurants and always enjoyed chatting with her. I knew she was doing a good job by the many ways that we measured and shared successes with our teams. One thing I truly remember about her is that she genuinely cared about what she did.

She contacted me because there was a high-level leadership position opening up at a company she'd been working at since leaving us.

She told me, "When I heard this position opened up and read the job description, I thought of you first." She continued, "The things I learned working with you have helped me so much in my life and with this current job. We are a family here, much like we were all those years ago." I was emotional. The "we" that we had created and instilled in our day-to-day operations had made such an impact on her life that she took the time to track me down and let me know about this opportunity—despite it being almost a decade since we last communicated.

So, there you have it—these things work. I hope I inspired you in many simple ways. The ideas in this book are not complicated and are really just basic concepts. But I had to learn through my own experiences and the teachings of others. So, enjoy my simple and to-the-point approach, and please try these ideas out in your own life. I promise they will improve things and help you "profit" through serving people—whatever "profit" means to you. Have a "Whopper" of a time!

DEDICATION

My pre-adulthood experiences could provide a laundry list of reasons why someone would not be successful. My father was absent from when I was three until I was twenty-seven. My siblings (a sister and two stepbrothers) and I grew up poor. My parents never spoke of college, I never went, and there wouldn't have been money for tuition. Throughout my life, I was teased because of my name, and I became the stepfather of a ten-year-old boy at the age of twenty-three.

All these challenges that could have been potential excuses for failure did the exact opposite; they turned into opportunities for me to prove that I could overcome them. I did not see them as reasons why I would fail. Instead, I viewed them as challenges, and I did everything in my power to maximize them.

There are many people in my life that I need to thank—too many, actually. I would like to begin by thanking my father, Bruno Hilgart Sr. It might be counterintuitive, but I really think I am in a better place today than I would be if he was in my life during my formative years. In many ways, my father was the polar opposite of me. May he rest in peace.

Thank you to my mother, Rita Armbrust. She had a unique way of parenting, but she loved me and always believed in me. This has always meant so much to me.

Thank you to my younger sister—who is only younger than me by 360 days—Tammy Rodriguez. She has always been my number one fan. She truly supports, respects, and—like my mother—believes in me. We are very close and always will be, even though we are many miles apart and do not talk to each other as much as we both would like to.

Thank you to my stepfather, Norm Armbrust, for the constant discipline and accountability. From curfew to finances, you taught me that there is a "responsible way of being irresponsible," even though you were rarely irresponsible yourself. By rarely ever drinking and never smoking, you taught me about clean living, and you were always proud to live within your means. You never tried to impress anyone and took crap from no one. You were the toughest dad among all my friends, and that was cool. May you rest in peace.

Thank you to my kids, Bill Conley, Kelly Hilgart, and Kevin Hilgart. You three are so different yet so much the same, loving me and respecting me as your dad. You have taught me not to take that role lightly and have always held me accountable. While I have had to learn the hard way many times, I did learn and will continue to learn from you because you are all such great kids. I could not be prouder of each of you.

Thank you to my wife, Mary Conley-Hilgart. You are everything to me. You have made me into the man I am today. I would not be writing this book without knowing you truly believe in me. You are my rock, my best friend, the mother of my children, and my lover. You are smart, witty, and make me look better in every situation. When people refer to you as my better half, they are so right. Who knows where I would be today without you—likely, nowhere near as great of a place as I am right now. We make a great team in so many ways, and you are admired by so many. We recently celebrated thirty-four years of marriage, and I look forward to many even better years ahead with the love of my life.

It would be remiss of me to go on without thanking one more person who made this book possible. William Gill was willing to take on the risk of opening his first business and gave me the opportunity to have a successful career. He also gave me the opportunity to meet my wife, Mary, when she started working with him as well. Throughout my time with you, Bill, I have gained so much experience and knowledge. You believed in people development and invested in me and my career growth. All of that has allowed me to become the businessman that I am today. Thank you for all your trust and support.

There are so many others—too many to mention—that have touched my life in some way. Thank you to every vendor, coworker, teammate, colleague, customer, peer, subordinate, boss, and competitor.

SPECIAL ACKNOWLEDGMENT TO ADITYA SHEKHAR

This project would never have happened if not for the totally random "chance" meeting I had with this young man.

I was between jobs and driving rideshare to pass the time. I picked up Aditya in Chicago on October 25, 2019. As often happened with passengers (at least 50 percent of the time), I began chatting with him as he sat in the back seat of my car. And it all started when I was asked a question passengers often asked: "do you drive rideshare full-time?"

I answered like I always did by saying, "For now, yes. But I spent thirty years managing Burger King restaurants and making people more passionate about salting french fries and preparing flame-grilled sandwiches than they ever thought possible."

He was taken by the conversation we subsequently had, which was focused on management and leadership. During this conversation, I came to find out he was a very educated, engaging, and inquisitive man who happened to have some writing and publishing experience. He let me get passionate about why there is a lack of good leaders in the workforce and how great companies understand the importance of people development.

Toward the end of the ride, my passenger asked me, "Have you ever thought about doing a TED Talk?"

I responded, "Yes, but I'm not sure how to make that happen." However, that question gave me the perfect opportunity to mention that I had been working on a book for almost eight years but was struggling to get it to the finish line. He then offered to take a look at what I had written so far.

In the three years since we met, we went chapter by chapter and added much more depth to the book. All along, he displayed what I learned about him on day one: he is wise beyond his years. He brought professionalism, readability, and coaching to the project. He also let me coach him on how to best edit my original work.

He walked a fine line between editing and not losing sight of the details, expertise, and passion of the author. We went back and forth about how to find the perfect balance between his language and my passion a few times, but we were always able to thread the needle.

In addition to helping me with the editing, he—more importantly—believed in me from the beginning. He knew that my perspective on leadership and passion for people development needed to get out to more people. He knew that my goal from the start of this book was to improve a world where so many leaders and managers are struggling because they were never taught how to manage and motivate others. And, when leaders and managers are struggling, their teams struggle too.

Aditya believed in me. He coached me, and he mentored me. He edited every word and sentence, and I could not be more grateful. Without him, this book would have never been finished. Thank you so much, Aditya (or, as I like to call him, Eddy).

www.ingramcontent.com/pod-product-compliance
Lightning Source LLC
LaVergne TN
LVHW041854070526
838199LV00045BB/1590